W A

PHOEBE SMITH

WAYFARER

Harper
North

HarperNorth
Windmill Green
24 Mount Street
Manchester M2 3NX

A division of
HarperCollins*Publishers*
1 London Bridge Street
London SE1 9GF

www.harpercollins.co.uk

HarperCollins*Publishers*
Macken House, 39/40 Mayor Street Upper
Dublin 1, D01 C9W8, Ireland

First published by HarperNorth in 2024

1 3 5 7 9 10 8 6 4 2

A catalogue record for this book
is available from the British Library

HB ISBN: 978-0-00-856652-4

Printed and bound in the UK using 100%
renewable electricity at CPI Group (UK) Ltd

To A for encouraging me to wander;
To B for bringing me back

A The Old Way
B John Bunyan Trail
C North Wales Pilgrim Way
D St. Columba's Way
E Whithorn Pilgrim Way
F St. Cuthbert's Way
G St. Peter's Way
H St. Michael's Way
I St. Hilda's Way
J Thames Pilgrim Way

NORTH

Hinderwell
Whitby
I

St. Andrews

Holy Island
Melrose F

Oban D
Mull
Iona

Newton
Stewart
E

NORTH ATLANTIC

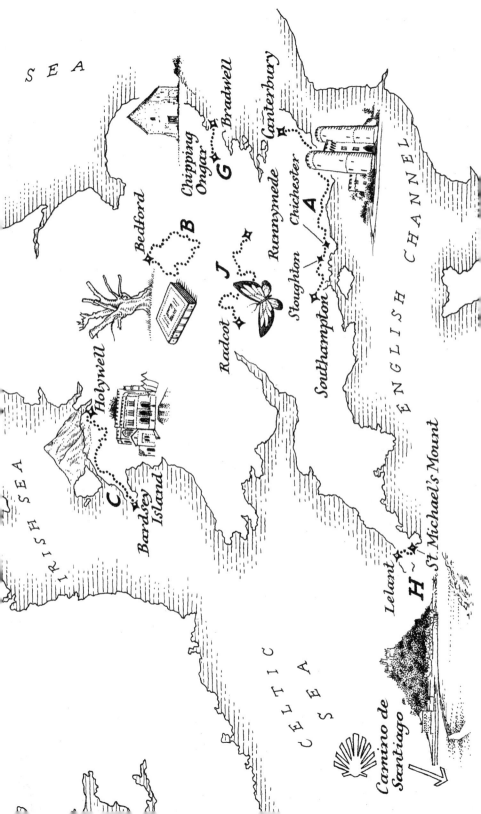

Contents

Author's Note

I have never been a religious soul. My dad is agnostic, and my mum was a lapsed Methodist. As the daughter of a miner, I suppose the idea of a religion that promises salvation for all rather than just the predestined elitist few appealed to Mum, and her family. She once told me that she decided to have me and my brother christened 'just in case', and I have vague memories of attending a Sunday school as a toddler – though I have a strong suspicion this was more to do with the free childcare it provided than a desire to have us taught the 'Word of the Lord'. All I remember was a yellow book with a rainbow on it (research subsequently led me to discover that this is the *Good News Bible*) and being allowed to eat two slightly soft biscuits in a draughty room with high beige ceilings and a carpet that scratched my legs when I sat on it.

Later, religion was part of the curriculum, as it is for most children. But I saw it as just that: part of the school timetable in the way that Maths and English were; a required subject to sit through and pass exams in. Of course, we had to say the Lord's Prayer before lessons, Grace before mealtimes and, in the autumn, someone would bake a particularly fancy bread product (I vividly recall a bale of hay with a little mouse on it) and we would bring in canned food for 'those in need' (we didn't have that much so I was always sent in with kidney beans and chickpeas that Mum seemed to buy once a year and never use). Come winter, we would stick candles into oranges to make Christingles without ever really knowing why. Looking back, I suppose religion was always there, though more of a backdrop to life than a key part of it.

The dichotomy of religion being a 'thing', rather than a subject to learn, hit me hard in my first year of high school, during an RE lesson with the Reverend Cook, and has stuck with me ever since. We had just come from double Biology, during which time I'd learned about evolution and seen skulls and fossils to prove the theory. I was taught how humans, like other creatures, have changed over time to adapt to conditions in their environment. I saw first-hand how whale fins still contain individual finger bones, an evolutionary remnant nodding to the fact that we share the same ancestors. It was a moment when questions I had about where we come from and how we got here clicked into place in my mind. The natural world and myself were genuinely connected. We were the same.

Dizzy from this revelation I went to my RE lesson. Here the story of Genesis – the creation of the universe by God – was being taught. I was eleven. It all sounded beautiful – the kind of magical story I would pen in my notebook to pass the time – but I was very confused.

In my innocence I asked the reverend: 'So where does this all fit in with the evolution of humans?' Was it, I postulated, that God created the monkeys that then became us over those seven days? Was it that one of those was Adam and the other Eve? That seemed to make the most sense to me, though it still didn't really add up in my head, and I had many questions.

I was instantly berated.

'I,' she said indignantly, 'did not come from any ape. Did you?'

'Well yes,' was my answer, 'we all did.'

That was what Miss Jones had literally just told us in Biology, I reminded her. I looked around at my classmates for support, someone to agree that I was in fact speaking the truth, but I was faced with blank stares or bowed heads.

From that point on, any interest in religion dissipated. It wasn't God that took it from me, it was Reverend Cook.

So when, many years later, I was sent on a work assignment to undertake a pilgrimage – perhaps one of the most fervent acts of devotion for many Christians – I never foresaw how much it would change, influence and even save my life. It may have been serendipity that took me to Spain to walk the Camino de Santiago, but it was a need to make sense of the world as a secular soul, to process past traumas, and to overcome loss, that drew me to Britain's forgotten spiritual trails. Along the way I carried my own beliefs, rather than those prescribed by someone else, and I urge you to do the same in the journey ahead.

Pre-amble

They say the Botafumeiro flies through the air in between the arches of Santiago Cathedral at speeds of over 42 mph. I watched as this huge golden vessel – just a few inches shorter than I am tall, and weighing only a little less than me – swooped above my head expelling the sweet scent of frankincense in plumes of smoke, while the melodious notes of a lone nun singing the 'Hymn to the Apostle' punctuated its oscillations.

For most pilgrims, this moment, after walking Spain's Camino de Santiago, is the culmination of weeks if not months of hiking and soul searching. It's a sign that a great voyage to find yourself, your deity, your own way in the world, has finally come to an end. It is markedly a joyous occasion whereby the pilgrim has completed something truly fulfilling, a kind of full stop at the end of a particularly satisfactory sentence.

And yet, for me, it wasn't any of those things.

As I watched the giant gold censer soaring through the air, I felt nauseous. Around me, pilgrims gasped in awe as this spectacle played out, while I remained silent. When it slowed to a pendulous, steady swing and was recaptured by the tiraboleiros (whose job it is to control its journey through the confines of the cathedral), I felt empty and lost. And I couldn't work out why.

So I went back. Three times over the course of the next thirty-six hours I was in the city. Each time I tried to pinpoint the hold the Botafumeiro seemed to have over me. When I was not stood gazing at it, I was thinking about it. Wandering around the city, I passed stores festooned with all manner of 'peregrino' paraphernalia – from Tarta de Santiago (a special pilgrims' almond cake with a dusting of icing sugar forming the shape of St James' cross), to scallop shells (representing the lines of the myriad routes pilgrims take to reach the cathedral) and dried-out gourds (a type of pumpkin that was used by medieval pilgrims to carry water, or sometimes, wine). They all seemed to blur together until they were nothing at all. I could no longer see them. Instead, I pictured that Botafumeiro; its curvaceous gilded chamber hemmed in by chains.

I had begun in Sarria, a town on a river of the same name, in the north-west of Spain's Galicia region. A little over 100 kilometres from the cathedral at Santiago, it is the most common starting point for pilgrims who want to gain a Compostela – the church-issued document that certifies the bearer as having completed the Santiago de Compostela and thereby grants forgiveness for all sins – in as little time as possible.

For me it was work – I was there as a travel writer, to walk it and write instructive articles for would-be pilgrims. As such, I approached it the same way I would any story I was writing. The first thing I did was research. And it was while doing this that I realised just how many paths there are that make up what is known as 'The Camino'. It's not just one thing, it is multiple. It can be started from your own doorstep, literally from anywhere in the world, but then, as you get closer to the final destination – the cathedral said to hold the remains of St James – there are several popular routes. These include the Camino Frances (the French Way, typically started in Saint-Jean-Pied-de-Port at the foot of the Pyrenees in France); the Camino del Norte (the Northern Way, usually begun from the coastal hub of San Sebastian); the Camino Português (the Portuguese Camino, starting at either Porto or Lisbon for those wanting a longer challenge); the Camino Primitivo (said to be the original Camino, walked by the 'founder' of the hike,

King Alfonso II, in the ninth century, beginning in the now little-known city of Oviedo that was once the former capital of the region); the Camino Inglés (aka the English Way, a route primarily used in medieval times by pilgrims coming from Britain, Ireland and northern Europe by boat, beginning in Spain from A Coruña or Ferrol); and the Vía de la Plata (an old trading route forged by the Romans, aka the Silver Way, which links the south and the north of Spain via a trail once used to transport precious metals from Seville).

But which is the official one? That seemed to be much debated across a plethora of forums. Though the Camino de Santiago has been around since the ninth century, when it was one of the top three destinations for pilgrims (the others being Rome and Jerusalem), it is only within the last few decades that it has enjoyed a resurgence in popularity.

Its origins date back to when Spain's patron saint (and one of Jesus' twelve apostles), James (or Sant Iago, hence 'Santiago' in Spanish), was beheaded in 44 AD by King Herod for preaching while in Jerusalem. It is said that his followers managed to miraculously repatriate his remains by stone boat and bury them in Spain, where they lay undiscovered for another 769 years. That was until, under Alfonso II's rule as King of Asturias (the north-western part of the country encompassing Cantabria, Castile Leon and what is known as Galicia) they were found.

There are several accounts of how the remains were unearthed, but the one I like the best reports that the king followed the lights of the Milky Way after getting a tip-off from a hermit, and found them after toiling on a trail over several days – thus becoming the first ever pilgrim to undertake the Camino.

It cannot be stressed enough just how important this discovery was for him. Already fighting to keep his region strong amid invasions from the south of the country, he was looking for a way to give his residents a firm cultural identity for which to keep fighting, and Alfonso's making his own the locality where something this precious could be found proved to be something of a marketing master-stroke. Not only did it give his area a claim to fame like those of Italy and the Middle East, but it gave people a reason to visit, bringing with them money and needs for hospitality – water, food, and a safe bed.

A couple of hundred years later its success had launched the publication of the *Codex Calixtinus* – essentially the first ever guidebook written to the route – the result of which saw pilgrims journey to the region from all over Europe and further afield. It spawned early souvenirs and even the enviable job of Professional (or Proxy) Pilgrim, who would be employed by the wealthy to walk the route for them, thereby gaining absolution of all sins without having to tread a single step.

The pilgrimage's popularity continued right up until the sixteenth century and the Reformation. Martin Luther, a former monk turned Augustinian friar in Germany, argued that pilgrimage was a dereliction of people's everyday duties and something of an indulgence. He also postulated that being able to gain a certificate of pardon was simply ludicrous. His views gained traction and were cemented and embraced in England when, thanks to good timing, King Henry VIII was keen to divorce his wife so he could marry someone else (an act forbidden by the prevailing religion). In 1538 he decided to break ways with the Catholic Church and ban all pilgrimages – an act that has still not officially been undone. Despite there having been calls over the last decade to remove the prohibition officially, the UK government has declined to get involved in such a potentially 'triggering' issue, given the religious connotations. This technically means that every step of making a British pilgrimage today is in some way tantalisingly illicit.

Banning pilgrimages had a dramatic impact on pilgrim numbers and had a huge impact on business within the previously booming region of Galicia. But, in the mid-1980s, around the time I was born, it all changed.

A man called Don Elías Valiña Sampedro, a pastor in O Cebreiro, sought to repopularise the Camino – in particular the route that ran alongside where he lived: the Camino Frances. In the nine years before he died, he was instrumental in organising the clearing of pathways that had become obstructed and lost to the undergrowth over the centuries, and set about waymarking the trail with painted arrows, which still survive today.

One source claims that he jumped into his Citroën GS to start in France with a large can of canary-yellow paint (the only colour he had to hand) and a big brush, and drove the entire route, stopping at key junctions to literally show people the way, telling bystanders that he was 'planning an invasion' (a phrase that landed him a night in the local police barracks).

He wasn't wrong, though. In 1984, when he started, the number of registered pilgrims who completed the Camino and earned their official Compostela was 423. By 2019 (pre-Covid), that figure had reached 347,578, with nearly 10,000 of them coming from the UK.

Despite there being multiple options for people to choose to walk, the oldest of the 'new' ones was definitely the Camino Frances. I – like readers of the articles I was writing for – didn't have weeks to dedicate to treading the trail from the mountains of France to the city of Santiago over 772 kilometres away. I needed to do the Camino in the quickest and most time-efficient way possible, which is when I discovered a loophole.

In 1993 a minimum-distance requirement was brought into force – not without controversy – to ensure that

11

people walking the Camino didn't literally stumble from their hotel room in Santiago post-breakfast and get absolution for a lifetime of sins. Instead, in another brilliant marketing initiative – certainly for those businesses that happened to fall within the designated distance – it was announced by the regional government of Galicia that as long as the last 100 kilometres was walked and a passport known as a *credencial* was stamped at various cafés, restaurants, hostels and churches along the way, the bearers could claim they had 'walked the Camino' and gain a Compostela from the cathedral office. You needn't be a mathematician to realise that the new ruling meant you can easily fit this most famous pilgrimage into a week's holiday – or five days of annual leave.

And so, I was posted to Sarria, the birthplace of the man who painted all the yellow arrows on the trail, to walk the last 100 kilometres of the Camino. Not for me, but for my readers.

Despite holding no belief in the power of gaining a Compostela, I reached Sarria feeling buoyed by the sunshine and relieved to be out of the office. For the past four years I had been working at the helm of a travel magazine and thrown myself into it on every level. I spent so much time trying to prove that I deserved the role that any social life I'd had in the previous three years was left in tatters. I regularly missed friends' birthdays, weddings and Christmas gatherings, so much so that I stopped being invited. My partner at the time was a photographer and most of the days we spent together we were working. If I wasn't already on assignment somewhere I was researching and planning to make it happen. I didn't just do the job, I was the job, and that was fine. Or so I thought.

I had arrived in Madrid by plane, which had been filled with a bachelor party in full swing. We were placed in a looping holding pattern for a full thirty minutes before landing, occasionally being pushed into a higher altitude by updraughts produced by the encircling mountains, before dropping thirty feet in a split second. Five of the passengers were sick; one was sitting next to me. By the time we made the final approach to the runway I could taste the acidic flavour of fresh vomit on my own tongue.

After taking the train to Sarria I spent the first evening practically waltzing through the flagstone streets, giddy with excitement at being away. I laughed at some of the garish Camino-themed tourist gifts, remarked on the prices of special Menu del Peregrinos (three courses and wine for under €10), and decided to visit a church for a special Pilgrim Mass.

The service was entirely in Spanish and I understood nothing, but I did opt to drink some of the offered wine and spent most of the prayers gazing at the domed ceilings, admiring the overly ornate reredos behind the altar, and trying to remember whether the person conducting the service should be called a priest or a vicar.

The following morning, I decided to take a bus and begin my walk from Samos, to warm up my legs post-travel and bolster my kilometre count from a hundred to at least fourteen above the minimum requirement.

Samos is home to a huge sixth-century monastery complete with cloisters straight out of Harry Potter's Hogwarts. It's run by a welcoming monk who looks every bit the Friar Tuck stereotype, with a big belly and huge, friendly smile. The building is as impressive as it is oppressive. Made of large lightly coloured granite, its façade dominates the entrance garden, and in essence the entire village, and a metal railing comprising large scallop shells denotes its indisputable link to the Camino.

I entered the building clutching my pilgrim passport, the *credencial* all Camino walkers must get stamped at regular intervals to prove they've walked it, looking fresh-faced and smelling clean. I was wearing a small orange backpack – which immediately singled me out from the other peregrinos who arrived seconds later, bearing huge loads along with the well-worn expressions of people who have been on the road for several weeks. Their faces were tanned, their cheeks rosy and they brought with them the distinct aroma of sweat that no amount of handwashing can ever quite remove. I'd smelt it a few months before when I'd been on assignment in the USA, interviewing 'thru-hikers' on the 3,500-kilometre Appalachian Trail. It lingered in every trail town establishment I visited, a distinct mixture of the sharpness of vinegar coupled with the sweetness of old ketchup.

They looked me up and down and I could tell from their expressions that I had immediately been summed up as a 'tourist' rather than a pilgrim. This was the first time I'd been found wanting, though it wouldn't be the last.

Some theorists argue that pilgrimage is, in itself, one of the earliest forms of tourism. The premise of a pilgrimage was to visit a place where there is a physical connection to a holy person or event, where old bones or remains are entombed or enshrined, or where a miracle is stated to have happened in a religious text or tradition. As such, the first destination for Christian pilgrims was Jerusalem – the Heavenly City, centre of the Holy Land, and the last link to the physical presence of Jesus Christ, who was buried there before he reportedly rose again.

One of the earliest records of a pilgrimage to Jerusalem is dated to 170 AD, when the Bishop of Sardis, in Turkey, called Melito, journeyed to the city and effectively went on a sightseeing mission aimed at connecting physical places to those written about in the Bible, thereby cementing its undisputable veracity. After him came the Roman Emperor Constantine, who ordered the building of a church over the burial site of Jesus and prompted other believers to follow in his footsteps. Shortly after him came a woman called Egeria in the fourth century. She is someone very few will have heard of, but she wrote arguably the first travelogue of a pilgrimage – way before the *Codex Calixtinus* was published – which at one point was even called *Itinerarium Egeriae* (meaning Travels of Egeria), though it was later changed to *Peregrinatio Aetheriae* (Pilgrimage of Aetheria).

That day I meandered along the Spanish country trails, collecting notes on this holy footpath as Egeria once did in Jerusalem. I watched cattle grazing nonchalantly, unconcerned by this lone walker on their land, and was greeted by an old couple still working on their acre with hand-pushed tools despite appearing well into their seventies. They stopped toiling as I passed and the man doffed his cap, revealing a balding head covered by wisps of black hair that flew free in the afternoon breeze. He uttered the words I had been waiting to hear since I arrived: 'Buen Camino' (have a good walk) – the typical greeting and parting utterance offered to pilgrims on The Way.

I forced a smile. After my run-in with the 'real' pilgrims that morning, I felt as though I was deceiving them. I felt like a cheat.

All the way back to Sarria my mind toyed with that word – cheat – tossing it around whenever my thoughts focused on something more agreeable. I heard the call of a cuckoo and stopped to listen closer, only to have the word 'cheat' echo in my head amid the silence. When I spied a cluster of wild poppies punctuating a field of green and stopped to take a photograph, it bounced back again, reverberating between my temples.

I'd come here as a traveller, never thinking I was a 'pilgrim', but now I was definitely disturbed not to be one, or to be called one when, in my head, I didn't deserve the moniker.

My inner critic continued to taunt me in the days that followed, shouting at me as I crossed the bridge into Portomarin on a particularly long and hot day, my foot already swimming in sticky serum as a blister formed and then popped into my sock. It provoked me again as I admired the Iron Age ruins at Castromaior and a group of ten fresh hikers cheerily called 'Buen Camino' at me while I drank my water; and it tormented me further when I reached Palas de Rei and sat down in a bar to enjoy a cold beer.

Next to me in the restaurant, pilgrims laughed about the number of people like me on the trail. They shared bold and gutsy stories of their experiences hiking over the Pyrenees, of hard-won victories securing a bed in popular albergues in dire weather, and of the satisfaction they were sure they would feel having 'really' walked the Camino once they reached Santiago.

Back on my own tourist trail, and attempting to silence my inner 'cheat', I threw myself into full journalist mode. I interviewed pilgrims at every turn, asking them how far they'd walked and why they were making the journey. The first few I spoke to had come from Sarria, and were doing it for the challenge, or purely as a walking holiday. But slowly I became more adept at distinguishing the 100-kilometre pilgrims from those who had been on the trail for weeks. It is often in the way they walk – effortlessly, faster, with no signs of blisters, the signifier of a body beaten into submission.

All those 'long haulers' I spoke to – without exception – were going through a major life change. Deaths, divorces, medical diagnoses or failure to get a job or a place in college. One woman had just lost everything in a house fire and felt that the only way to take the emotional first step back into what her new life would be was to take a physical step into the unknown, with some unknowns. She had started walking the Camino solo, but now had a group of friends around her from all over the world. The Camino had given these people time to adjust to a new situation, and space to ask themselves questions about what they wanted to do next.

Outside the tiny enclave of A Rúa, on the second-to-last day on the trail, around 25 kilometres from Santiago, I met a father and daughter at a small trailside café. He was in his late sixties, a similar age to my own dad at the time, and she was in her thirties. They had decided to walk The Way together after he retired and his partner, her mother, had sadly died. Their affection for each other was obvious, with a near-silent respect demonstrated by a slow, agreeing nod, or the brush of a forearm when one of them was recounting a particularly tough section of their journey from St Jean in France.

I sat and listened to their tales, and thought of my own father. In the years since we'd lost my mum to cancer in 2001, our relationship had become distant and somewhat strained. My career had sapped my focus, and his other, newer relationships had seemed to push ours to the periphery. The idea that I could ever persuade him to spend time with me like this felt implausibly remote.

Feeling myself beginning to choke up, I made an inane joke about taking it easy in retirement and hastily got back on the trail. As the chestnut trees rose up around me, I attempted to squash my feelings into the size of a nut and swallow them away. A trickle of water splashed off the foliage and onto my face, before being joined by more raindrops. The heavens had decided to open, and I ran the last kilometre of the day to escape the torrent of whatever was coming.

The final section of the Camino saw the mood of my fellow walkers shift. As the woodland paths gave way to more tarmac roads, people seemed quicker to take out their phones, playing music loudly and abandoning quiet reverence for loud exclamations of whatever emotion was passing at the time.

I, on the other hand, had already begun to retreat inside myself. I had stopped interviewing pilgrims. I didn't want to be part of their world. Before I knew it, I had made it to Monte do Gozo (the Hill of Joy), the place where pilgrims would rapturously glimpse their final destination. But my climb was devoid of enjoyment.

I left the trail to find the statues of two pilgrims pointing in the direction of the city, fashioned by Galician sculptor José Acuña in 1993. As they stand a five-minute walk off the main pathway, very few peregrinos see these figures, but this is the only spot from which you can truly get that first look at the cathedral.

As I reached it the rain arrived once more. I looked out to see the grey shapes of the spires – encased in scaffolding for structural repairs. Even my 'joyous', view was obscured.

I took off my boot; another blister had formed. I tried to pop it with the pen from my notebook. After several attempts, my skin finally relented and the serum oozed out. I winced, but was strangely relieved that I could feel something, even if it was a stinging pain.

My final steps into the city were once more accompanied by the word 'cheat' pulsating in my head. Every footstep I took, even with the discomfort of the burst blister, felt like a lie.

As I neared my final goal more tourists emerged, pounding the pavement. We wore identical scallop shells, which bounced with each footstep. An early symbol of a 'true pilgrim', they can now be bought from one of the souvenir stalls in Sarria. We were headed not to the cathedral and the claimed final resting place of St James but rather to the Pilgrims' Office to get our Compostelas.

My fellow tourists and I now outnumbered the true peregrinos and I hated myself for being one of them. I had the right clothes, the right 'look', the right expression on my face, even authentic injuries. And soon I held the actual Compostela, written in Latin, in my hand. But this wasn't real. I wasn't real.

My last attempt to decipher why the Botafumeiro made me feel the way it did came on the morning I caught the train back to Madrid. I woke early and went back to the cathedral. Although the swinging of the censer is only for special occasions (or, as I would later discover, a reward for a large donation), when I arrived – along with a fresh batch of pilgrims – it was already in full swing.

Back in the early days of pilgrimage to Santiago, it's believed that they burned the incense to purify the air of the cathedral, air that would have been fairly rancid as more and more dirty peregrinos crammed inside. Now, as we all watched the arc of this ornate vessel, packed with so many expectations and a promise to make things better, I realised its great contradiction. It was at once moving at great speed yet stuck, trapped in the confines of the cathedral. A beautiful place to be, but anywhere can be a prison if you find you cannot get out.

I was that Botafumeiro. I was the vessel carrying so many expectations and hopes inside me, trying my best to put on the best show every time, to not let anyone down – from my lost mother, to my employer, my partner and my readers – travelling through life fast and excitedly, yet all the while I was doing it I was confined to a space I'd created, one with no place else left to go. One where others were controlling what happened next, and could bring it all to a halt with the simple tug of a rope over which I had no control.

Something had to change.

I left the cathedral looking back only once. As I did, my eyes fixed on the rooftop. Up there, with a saint's-eye view down onto the Plaza de Platerías, is the simple stone trough beneath the bronze Cruz dos Farrapos – the cross of the rags. It's here that medieval pilgrims are said to have burned their clothes, symbolically ending their old life so they could begin a new one.

I didn't realise it as I left Santiago, but not long after I returned home I was going to start a fire of my own.

ONE

The Old Way

It is spring again – May. A full year has passed since I
walked the Camino in Spain and now I find myself, once
more, on another, unexpected, spiritual trail in the heart-
land of Kent, a county in England where my own father was
born many years ago.

It's not yet dawn, but I am wide awake, lying on a pile of
stacked prayer cushions, swaddled in my sleeping bag, in
front of an altar that's emblazoned with the words 'Grant
us thy peace'. Above me a gold cross stands tall, flanked by
two unlit candles, and a vaulted ceiling disappears into the
darkness of an early morning not yet touched by the light
of the sun.

Amid the many rows of pews I hear the gentle snores of
the pilgrims with whom I have shared this journey for the
last three days. Everything is quiet and still. But I am restless, plagued by uncomfortable memories.

Suddenly the silence is shattered by fits of laughter. Four women emerge through the church vestibule, naked, wrapped only in towels. With no showers on the trail, it had been suggested to them the previous evening that they could bathe in the early-morning dew as pilgrims would have done in the past. Seeing the sun slowly rising between stones in the graveyard outside has apparently been impossible for them to resist.

They are trying to whisper, but are so overcome with exhilaration that they're almost shouting.

'I filmed it,' says one, between chortles, 'but I don't have to post it anywhere.'

'Oh I don't care,' says another. 'It was just such a beautiful moment I don't mind who sees it.'

'Agreed,' chimes another and they all burst into further fits of laughter.

I can't define what I feel hearing this. In the past I might have been concerned they would later regret their actions. But perhaps that censorious instinct was a hangover from previous relationships. The men I'd known would never have allowed me to do something like that, through a look, a squeeze of my wrist, or a slight tilt of the head that implied there would be consequences.

I close my eyes and turn away. These women are not like me.

The room was spinning. I'd drunk more than I should. By design rather than mistake.

I knew that when we arrived back at our room there would be an expectation for certain things to happen. It was his birthday after all. And so I had drunk the wine as though it were water.

Dutifully I prepared myself for the inevitable; he was my boyfriend, after all. I looked over to the yellowing blinds in the hotel-room window; they were coated in a thick film of dust and sagged to one side awkwardly. A single tug would probably see them completely fall apart.

Then, it started.

I went through the motions, did what I was meant to do. Forced a smile, then pressed him to my chest so that he couldn't see my face, nor I his.

I didn't want it. Yet I was letting it happen to me.

I trained my eyes on the chink of light slicing into the room through a gap in the broken blinds and tried to imagine myself outside the window, a passer-by on the pavement, unaware of what was happening inside.

Then the pain came.

I couldn't bear it. So I said so. Once. Twice. But nothing was changing, in fact it was becoming more intense. A sharpness tore through me.

I pleaded to make it stop, I tried to push him away, but I wasn't strong enough.

My whole body withdrew, stopped fighting, allowed it to continue, because then at least I knew it would be over quicker.

'What's wrong with you?' he asked as he pulled away.

I hadn't noticed but tears were streaming down my face. I was embarrassed. And hurriedly wiped them away.

'I can't believe you tried to make me a rapist,' he said, before adding, under his breath, 'and on my birthday too.'

My romantic relationships have always been torrid. One of my earliest, in particular, had felt like a challenge from the start. Everyone was against it, rooting for it not to work. My dad even boasted: 'I won't say "I told you so" when this all goes wrong.'

And so I became stubborn, determined to silence the naysayers and the doubters. Our love was fuelled by passion and turbulence. At the start it was exciting – the arguments felt electric. And, even a few months in, when he hit me and a visible bruise meant I had to change my hairstyle to hide my face, I made excuses for his behaviour. He blamed me and so did I – it was because of the things I'd said, things I'd done. When it happened again I was ashamed to tell anyone – I never thought being a victim of domestic abuse could happen to a strong woman like me. So I told myself I could take it – all of it – and on some level I reasoned that if I did then it meant someone else didn't have to.

I couldn't let anyone see past the gilded version of our love. Being the only one who knew about the violence meant it was a secret that I controlled, and in a perverse way I allowed myself to feel strong and potent. I vowed I would take it with me to the grave.

As time moved on and people no longer ventured opinions, the secret became less of a hidden amulet and more of a weighted burden. To make it work I had given up friends, having been convinced they were out to sabotage us. I stopped going out to avoid the inevitable arguments afterwards. I gave up socialising. I stopped drinking, having been told by my partner that it made me act in a way that I shouldn't. Everything I did was perfectly, 'lovingly' controlled. I oscillated between work and home; my life was a pendulous swing: fast and exciting in some ways, monotonous in others. Everyone I met told me I 'had it all'. I was not the kind of woman who needed help, and no one would ever ask if I was okay. When I miraculously got out I swore I would never allow such coercion to happen again.

In my latest relationship, to all appearances everything was fine: my career was thriving and we were both settled. Settled but stale. Where once I was controlled, now I felt pressure to take the reins and make things work. We never went out; no meals, no drinks, no friends. On my birthday I had to beg to go somewhere, and even then I had to organise it myself. I was convinced this was all I deserved.

My unconscious need for change started with a gradual shift so subtle I didn't even realise it was happening at all. It began with food. I didn't do anything dramatic, didn't secretly sneak off to the bathroom and make myself sick. I simply stopped eating.

At first, I skipped meals or only picked at what I was given. I started drinking coffee instead. Whenever I felt the urge to eat I'd boil the kettle. When that no longer hit the spot, I started putting sugar in it and very little milk. The bitterness tasted good. If people asked why I wasn't eating, I simply said I felt unwell.

After just a few weeks my trousers became loose; after nearly two months I could take off my jeans without undoing them. I knew it wasn't a good thing, but it felt incredible. Every time I slipped out of them with the zip still closed I felt a rush of exhilaration, a sort of sordid achievement. People began to compliment me on how good I looked. I noticed I now had a gap between my usually wobbly thighs. So I upped my exercise regime too. Every lunchtime I went to the gym, swam, did weights, cycled. When I felt the pang of hunger scratching away in my belly I convinced myself it was a prized accolade, the reward for all my dedication.

As I controlled what went into my body, I somehow felt I'd regained control of everything else. I stopped heading home after the office closed and started going out to any and all work events, and when I was there I would drink wine and cocktails – it wouldn't take many in my newly tiny form to make me forget my problems.

But soon, physical signs made it visibly clear I wasn't well. My hair became brittle, my gums began to recede, my nails broke, and I found it increasingly difficult to concentrate.

One day at work, while making yet another cup of coffee, a colleague followed me into the kitchen and shut the door behind me. 'Are you okay?' they asked.

The question threw me. I thought I could answer it confidently, but my body betrayed me before I could speak. I started crying uncontrollably.

Something had to change, starting with my unhappy relationship. That night was the last he slept in the house.

The invitation that arrives on my desk is marked BYOB, a repurposed acronym devised by the recently formed British Pilgrimage Trust (BPT), meaning Bring Your Own Beliefs. Set up by Will Parsons and Guy Hayward in 2014 as a way of resurrecting the lost art of pilgrimage, the BPT is a charity that guides people on ancient pilgrim trails to holy places – be they the standard churches and chapels or, very often, sacred trees, burial mounds and secret water sources. I am newly single and in a state of limbo, readjusting to life on my own, rattling around in an empty house. I no longer feel I have the energy to throw myself into work in the way that has helped me in the past. So I decide, on a whim, to join this trip. It's in the guise of work – I will write an article about their project – but in truth it's actually something I want to do for myself.

I meet them uncharacteristically early in Hamstreet in Kent, where they tell me they are trying to re-establish an ancient route they have discovered on a medieval document that may date back as far as the reign of Edward I: the Gough Map.

When I was younger, I hated maps. For someone who is more comfortable around words than numbers, they seemed too technical, too rigid. Yet as I grew older, I began to see the beauty in maps, especially those featuring Wales, the place of my childhood. The names of features on the landscape here are often poetic rather than functionary. The meaning behind a lot of Welsh phrases tells you more about how the area was interpreted by locals than any numbers can. For instance, Afon Goch means 'red river', after the iron leaching from the hills that turns the surrounding rocks of the banks rust-red. Yr Wyddfa, as Snowdon is now known, means 'grave' or 'burial mound'.

Local lore says it is the final resting place for the giant Rhita Gawr, who wore a cloak of beards taken from the thirty kings he defeated before he was slain by King Arthur and covered with cairns that make up the summit. It's a fitting tale and name for the nation's highest peak.

When Will and Guy show me a copy of the Gough Map, I'm surprised to see that this ancient chart is less grid squares and contour lines, and more illustrative artwork. Coloured white and red, with gold lettering for some cities, it features little drawings of houses and – most distinctly – churches, defined by their spires. Its origins are unclear, though it's thought to date from the late medieval period, at best guess around 1366. The name comes from the man – Richard Gough – who donated it to a library in 1809.

Scholars write about the inaccuracies of the document – the oversizing of some areas of England and Wales, the complete lack of knowledge surrounding Scotland, and references to mythical figures, such as Brutus of Troy (a Trojan warrior said to have founded Britain when he landed on the shores of Devon), passed off as fact. But all those things make me love it even more. What interested Will and Guy the most, however, were the red lines on the map that appeared to link places together, including old roads and footpaths. One in particular stood out: the route that appeared to join Southampton with the cathedral in Canterbury.

'It not only starts at a church and ends at the cathedral – which is a known ancient pilgrim site,' says Will while we wait for other pilgrims to arrive in a small patch of woodland on a sunny Saturday morning, 'but looking at it closely you can see that it stops at more churches and holy places along the way.'

To Will this was a sign – he was looking for evidence of the oldest pilgrim route known to have been walked in Britain and he had found it. He and Guy, keen to re-establish the trail, gave it a name, 'The Old Way', and began to transpose the Gough Map onto the most recent Ordnance Survey map to create a new footpath that utilised existing rights of way and bridleways. They hope that this 386-kilometre journey might become as popular as the Camino de Santiago in Spain.

This walk we're about to start will be one of a series of guided two- and three-day sections of the entire pathway. They ask participating pilgrims for donations, and use the experience as a way to check the route as they go.

By now I am the thinnest I've ever been in my life. Even my fleece, which normally makes me look chunky, hangs off my minuscule frame in folds. On my way to Kent I work up the courage to tell my dad that my most recent relationship is over. Instead of 'I told you so' there is just concern and an offer to come to see me. I am shocked by his reaction, and quickly decline.

As I stand patiently waiting for the others, I feel pretty sceptical that walking three days with a group of strangers is going to help me. After all, on the most famous pilgrimage in the world – one where people traditionally go to find themselves – I had lost my way. But as I am slowly joined by another thirty-four souls, I realise there is no backing out now.

As I often do in uncomfortable situations, I take out my notebook and pen. There's something about having this little leatherbound cluster of pages in my hand at any given time that helps me feel as though I am untouchable. It's my pocket-sized shield: I can take it out and write something – anything – into its pages and instantly remove myself from the scene. When using it I become almost invisible. Like I'm there, but not really.

Others are more at ease, more forthcoming. A woman, also alone, walks over and introduces herself as an artist living in a commune. Unprompted, she shares with me how she has been in an 'on again, off again' relationship with a wildlife guide who is messing her around and confesses that she has come for a break from the emotional rollercoaster she feels she is riding on.

Will approaches us, clutching two wooden staffs that he has coppiced himself from hazel. He tells us that he uses hazel as his go-to material as it's flexible and strong and tends to grow fairly straight. Though it seems counterintuitive, apparently by cutting off a branch from a great, wise tree, you can sometimes extend its life rather than shorten it (a tree left alone will live to about eighty, yet coppiced hazel can thrive for hundreds of years). He offers a staff to each of us.

'They will start off heavy,' he explains as the weight pulls my hand down towards the earth with an unexpected jolt, 'but over time, they do lighten.'

We swap staffs to see how they compare. Mine is definitely heavier, but I feel it has been handed to me for a reason. So I resign myself to trudging my way along this route with aching arms.

It turns out there are quite a few people here who feel in need of a little help to find their way. There are couples and groups of friends, a mother and daughter, and a handful of solo women and men, who each drip-feed me information about the events that have led them here. One arrives wearing thick layers of blue cloth – a bana – and a turban draped with more navy blue folds. Though white and British, she introduces herself to me with a Sikh name.

Acquaintances made, Will and Guy begin to explain how this experience is designed to allow our minds and bodies to reconnect at the same pace, away from the clamour of day-to-day life. And with that, we begin walking.

The ground is hardened into ridges of previously pliable mud in the unseasonable heat of the morning. We step over them in a messy cluster of bodies, not yet accustomed to walking in a throng. Pockets of conversation begin to explode like flowers blooming in the dawn. I linger near the back, purposely setting myself apart from the group. Slowly, I wander amid the broad-leaf trees of this tiny fragment of prehistoric woodland that sits as a reminder that at one time most of the Weald – the 193-kilometre by 48-kilometre stretch of land between the Kent marshes and the New Forest in Hampshire – was covered by trees.

Soon we reach a church in Ruckinge, a Norman-built offering with the usual square tower, topped with a pyramidal roof and needle spire. Already we are ushered in for tea and cake. Typically, I hold fast and go back outside to look at a sign installed by the Ordnance Survey, designating a spot in the graveyard as being the site where, in 1790, the distance between the observatories in Greenwich and Paris was first calculated.

Now refreshed, the group continue to follow a route occasionally marked as the Saxon Shore Way. Before long we are marching in a near-perfect line along the Royal Military Canal, heading east. This manmade structure feels as far from a natural waterway as it gets, yet around six thousand years ago we would have been walking along sea cliffs, with the waves of the Channel crashing beneath our feet.

That prehistoric coastline is now Romney Marsh, land reclaimed by our Roman ancestors to produce more food for a burgeoning population. In an effort to duel with nature, dykes were dug, sea walls constructed and the land drained. Later, another battle was anticipated – though not between the natural world and the industrial one. This time it was the 1800s and war with Napoleon had leaders worried that an invasion was imminent. So the canal was created, at a cost that in today's money would be around the £10 million mark. Any soil removed in the construction of the waterway was built up to form a makeshift parapet on the landward side. On the seaward edge, kinks were placed at regular intervals to allow cannons to be placed, while a lower towpath was maintained to enable horses to move loads along the canal.

We leave this landmark to head uphill to another church, at Bilsington, where Guy and Will decide to lead everyone in song. I sit, accidentally and awkwardly, in a corner of a pew abutting two women who sing loudly and fairly tunelessly. I admire their confidence.

In the seaside town of North Wales where I grew up there was a nightclub for those people who never really fitted in. Whereas the other clubs traded on white bars, wipe-clean floors and humorously named cocktails, this one, called The Bistro, was unashamedly styled to be a cross between someone's living room and a 1970s pub. The walls were covered with flock wallpaper that long ago had been crudely painted over with thick pink emulsion. The carpets were sticky with spilled drinks, each footstep accompanied by the sound of tearing fibres.

One end was for the Indie-rock kids, with tuneful guitar-led hits pumping out below spinning lights, edged by purple-cushioned booths and rickety chequered stools. The other was for those who had taken something to make the night go a little faster. There the music was up-tempo, with heart-shaking beats and a black light that made everyone's teeth glow fluorescent white.

It was the place of many firsts for me. First drink, first kiss (in the girls' toilets with a man called Paul). And it was also the venue where I first sang in public.

Back then (though I didn't know it at the time) I was clumsy and awkward in my own skin, but free of pretty much everything else: inhibition, self-doubt and anyone controlling my actions. I joined a band, dyed my hair green and blue with a thick streak of platinum at the front, and hung out with a long-haired guitarist called Dave in his backstreet flat that stank of his Berkeley Red cigarettes. I was constantly told I would never leave this town, that people like me would stay here forever. I didn't fight it – I revelled in its certainty.

My band was called Euphoria and for the first time, away from the ludicrously pretty girls in my high school with their perfect nails and magazine-styled make-up and hair, I felt I belonged somewhere. I could rock up with unbrushed, greasy hair, a slut collar ironically draped around my neck and last night's smudged eyeliner halfway up my cheek, and I would be accepted. We were a jumble sale of a band. There was one guitarist who had so many anxiety issues, and drug dependencies, that he barely spoke, but he made his instrument sing in unrivalled harmonics. The other was a window cleaner who worked with his dad, seemingly just there because there was nothing else to do in his village. Our bassist dealt drugs and sold the *Big Issue* and our drummer had a proper job at a university, where he was a technician. He'd recently traded his long, curly hair for a buzz cut after falling in love with a girl.

Our songs were packed with pitch and tempo changes and a hodgepodge of lyrics, penned by me, that paired 'profound' metaphors within nonsensical stanzas that just sounded good.

When I sang with them I felt invincible.

I never would have believed it if you'd have told me then that twenty years later I'd be in a church with just a clutch of other people, unable to find my voice.

'So, you're a singer, who can't sing?' asks Will later that day. We are making offerings to a holy well above a farm, which to me appears as little more than a bog punctuated with stinging nettles. He has a strange knack for making me feel utterly uncomfortable and completely at ease at the same time. He has a colourful past himself: having left university he decided to go for a walk and, in his words, 'accidentally became a wandering minstrel', singing for his supper for close to a year before his friends left their life on the road behind, settled down, and Will was cast aside, still wandering, and wondering what was next. I wasn't sure that I even liked him at first; I often found his questions intrusive rather than curious. Yet, somehow, on the top of a hill in Kent, he gets me to confess that since I had my first proper relationship years ago and left my band I'd never been able to sing in public again. Secrets of my past continue to gush out of me to this near stranger and it is difficult to make them stop.

We finish the day wandering along the edge of Port Lympne Safari Park. My position in this group of walkers has now changed; I no longer linger at the back by myself, but somehow find my way into the middle. Beside me a pack of African wild dogs suddenly emerge behind a flimsy wire fence, barking at the pilgrims who pass them. While others jump, scream and run ahead, I keep walking at my own pace, snarling back at them, feeling an unfamiliar safety within my own temporary herd.

That night we arrive at Saltwood Castle, a large stone fort, now in private hands, which sits on a site thought to have been fortified since the fifth century. It is famous, Will and Guy tell us – among pilgrims at least – as being the location from where the knights Reginald FitzUrse, William de Tracy, Hugh de Morville and Richard le Bret, incited by an enraged outburst by King Henry II ('who will rid me of this turbulent priest?'), plotted and then set off to murder Thomas Becket on a December night in 1170.

At school, history never grabbed my attention. All we were taught seemed to be centred around Henry VIII's many wives or the Second World War. Women were either being knocked up and beheaded or not mentioned at all. So my working knowledge is a bit thin, but a surreptitious bit of research on my phone confirms that Becket was a former friend of the king, who had come from very little and risen to the role of Archbishop of Canterbury and, simultaneously, Chancellor (a shrewd move doubtlessly designed by His Majesty to control the Church and, with it, the country). Resigning from the latter without telling the King caused their friendship to falter and led Becket to be exiled to France. Under what turned out to be a false promise of protection, he returned to England only to be gruesomely murdered in Canterbury Cathedral.

The moral of the story seemed to be that if you rise above your station and stand up to those in power you will – quite literally – be smited. Though, I note, the story did end with a twist. On his death, Becket was canonised by the

Pope as a saint and soon miracles were reported by those who visited his tomb. Coming to pay respects to him became the pilgrimage of the century and images of his murder still adorn church walls in Germany, Italy, Spain and Norway to this day. He became a legend in Europe as a defender of the Church. In fact, so revered was he that the king himself, who had played a part in his death, had to plead forgiveness at his tomb, having walked barefoot through the streets of Kent to the cathedral wearing a plain wool shirt and voluntarily being struck and whipped by monks. Becket's body was moved out of the crypt to a glitzy shrine and for years his resting place became an important ecclesiastical destination. And now, here we are following in their footsteps nearly nine hundred and fifty years later.

The castle at Saltwood is now occupied by a single woman, a widow called Jane Clark, who inherited the place from her father-in-law – via her late husband, the Tory MP Alan Clark. She gives us permission to camp in the grounds and promises to show us into the castle the following day.

My camping is usually done on a mountain top or deep in the wilderness, alone and away from anyone. For years I've sought solace in the outdoors, revelled in its ability to level the playing field. Rain, I believe, falls the same on all of us. Ever since I spent that first night on my own under stars more than fifteen years ago, and felt an unfamiliar rush of freedom, camping has been something of a salvation for me amid the stress of work and the most tempestuous relationships. People often think me strange for doing it by myself, but over the years it has been a necessity rather than a hobby. It's a time when I alone get to hold the map, I choose the pathway and I decide where I should spend the night. I have never requested permission to sleep amid nature and never sought the comfort of others to do it safely. Yet here I am, with a group larger than any I've ever walked with before, about to sleep, legally, on a rich person's estate. I feel like Becket must have done, moving amid people from a world he knew nothing about.

That night I surprise myself, and Will too, I think. Everyone imagines I will choose a place to camp well away from the group, but I find myself unexpectedly craving company. I head into the large white marquee that has been erected for us on the grass and bag a corner right at the back. That night I sleep better than I have for months, surrounded by the snores of thirty-odd strangers and hemmed in by the blank canvas walls.

The scream of a peacock wakes me at dawn. I sit bolt upright in my sleeping bag, temporarily confused as to where I am. In the weeks leading up to this trip my sleep has fallen somewhere between broken and non-existent. I have thrown myself into work until I have become too physically tired to continue, but when finally in bed I have spent hours lying awake, running through my actions of the last few months, feeling guilty about hurting my ex. For as long as I can remember I've worked so hard at taking any burden from others that doing the opposite feels despicably selfish. I stayed with a violent ex to avoid upsetting him, didn't tell my family what he'd done in case they felt guilty about not knowing or helping. I'd remained in an unhappy relationship so as not to shatter other people's illusion that you could have the 'perfect' life. I'd allowed my family to believe I was coping following my mum's death, to remove any concern. Now, by ending a relationship so suddenly, I had upset everyone. I can't shake the feeling that if only I'd stayed put, if I'd have just let things be, only one person would have been upset – me – and that is something I have grown more than accustomed to.

All these intrusive thoughts return in a violent cascade that morning and I am eager to start walking again. Most of the pilgrims I speak to say they walk so that they have time to think. Personally, I find the opposite is true: I don't think at all, I just am. I am the foot placements and handholds I seek, I am ducking under branches or climbing over fallen trees, I am standing on a mountain top, I am marvelling at the wind that pulls at my hair. I am my actions and I am most firmly in the world, rather than inside my own head.

But first, I have to endure the promised tour of the castle. All the talk of violence and betrayal is too much for me, so I stick close to Jane instead, to hear her tales of living in such an historic place. She leads me up some stone steps into her library, a grand room filled with towering bookshelves and huge timber tables, bathed in the hazy glow of many lancet windows. Immediately I feel calm as the earthy scent of old paper fills my nostrils.

If you look up Jane's late husband there is a string of colourful stories about him, of the affairs she had to endure even from the day she married him aged just sixteen (he was thirty-two and apparently took a mistress on their honeymoon). I wonder if she ever wished she'd left him. I want to ask her why she stayed and whether it had been the right decision, but instead I say nothing.

Before we leave, she tells me that there is one part of the castle she won't ever enter, occupied by a restless spirit. She says that she decided long ago to lock it away and leave it to its own devices. She is happy to surrender part of her home for it to exist in a place separate from her. Jane doesn't strike me as a woman who believes in the supernatural, but she says it so matter-of-factly that it is difficult to doubt her assertion. It seems that even those for whom death is the end of a relationship can't escape the ghosts of the past.

We depart in the footsteps of the murderous knights, but in place of bloodlust I feel the first pangs of hunger

I've had for a while. Following the Elham Valley Way up to the top of Tolsford Hill, I notice one of my fellow pilgrims looks frustrated, constantly annoyed with everyone and everything. Others in the group dismiss her as trouble, but I recognise something in her eyes: a loss or emptiness. She needs to be there as much as anyone else. I learn that she had once been a public figure and converted to Sikhism for her husband, who left her only a few months later. I wonder how many others in the group have compartmentalised trauma that's beginning to drip out like spilled blood on this ancient and troubled trail.

From the top of the hill I get my final glimpse of the coast and watch as a train disappears into the Channel Tunnel, bound for foreign lands. If I had been standing here months earlier, I would have desperately envied the passengers on that train for escaping to somewhere more exotic. But at this moment, something tells me I am exactly where I need to be.

Some of the things we do on this pilgrimage do seem silly or indulgent to me. Leaving silver pins as offerings at Hall Downs; resting our heads on the walls of the churches we pass to 'feel their energy'; and sitting for more than forty minutes amid bluebells in Bedlam Woods. I am frustrated by the pace. I itch to get moving.

'Pilgrimage is all about slowing down,' Will tells me as we walk now, at the front of the group, through an old

Saxon holloway, beside an avenue of black poplar trees. We reach the top of a hillside before anyone else joins us and he asks if he can take a picture of me. Reluctantly, I agree, but when he shows me the photograph I barely recognise my thin face. I feel exposed. I am surprised by how big my clothes look on me. If I lose any more weight, I wonder, would I disappear completely?

Our final evening sees us all overnight inside the medieval church at Barham.

'Yes – literally anywhere,' says Will, when I ask if I can lay my camping mat down beneath the altar.

From the look on some pilgrims' faces they believe that my chosen resting place is disrespectful, but I feel an inexplicable need to be as close to the sacred epicentre of the building as possible. And for once I decide to risk others' disdain.

'Pilgrimage isn't about religion,' Will tells me later, as our group decamps to the local pub to celebrate nearing our final day on the trail. 'The word's origin has been muddled over time, and people have assumed it must be something it isn't.'

He explains how 'pilgrimage' comes from the Latin '*per agri*', meaning 'through the field' and '*peregrinus*', meaning 'stranger'. 'It's just another way to describe walkers,' he assures me, 'so everyone is welcome on a pilgrimage; it doesn't matter what you do or don't believe.'

When the giggling bathers return to the church that morning, full of life and exhilaration at their carefree naked deed, I lie still trying to work out why it bothers me so much. I am not a meek or shy person. Anyone who's met me would laugh at the suggestion. Yet for what seems an entire lifetime I have been playing a part, smiling when I need to, holding back on my own desires, while submitting to those of others. When that behaviour began I couldn't say, but pretending to be happy has become such a part of me for so long that I am not really sure how much of the real me – the one who wants things for herself – remains.

I sit up and congratulate the women on their daring escapade, even though what I really feel now is hurt. Hurt that no one thought to ask me if I'd like to be a part of it. And also envy: that they had found ease in each other's company and in their own skin.

On the final day's walk we follow the remains of a Victorian railway line, stopping at a mural-rich fourteenth-century church at Bishopsbourne – replete with medieval graffiti carved into the stone pillars that keep it standing – and continue onwards to Canterbury in the hope we make it in time for Evensong. As we near the city, signage bearing the icon of a pilgrim begins to appear along the route.

Guy explains that we are now following the Pilgrims' Way, a well-established walking route between Winchester and Canterbury, much of it beside several motorways (including the M25, M26 and M20).

'Our route, The Old Way, is an alternative, more rural, way to get to Becket's grave,' says Guy. 'It's our hope that eventually we will have our own waymarking, passports and even a Compostela equivalent for finishers.'

Until he says it I haven't even considered the idea. On the Camino it was the carrot dangled in front of you that obliged you to complete a minimum distance, yet here, over three days in which we must have covered at least half of those kilometres, we are doing it for nothing at all – just the journey itself. I wonder how different an experience it would have been had we needed to collect stamps for a *credencial* or worry about how long the queue would be for the coveted certificate at the end.

I realise then that, for the past forty-eight hours, I have unknowingly relinquished my usual journalistic control and forgotten about the article I am supposed to be writing. I have morphed from impartial observer to immersed participant without even noticing. I feel in my pocket for the reassuring shape of my notebook and begin to scribble down some words, desperately trying to revert to my default character. Getting this close to my subject was never part of the plan, and now it feels reckless. I make a conscious effort to move to the back of the pilgrim pack, and fall a few steps behind everyone else, adding physical distance between us, even if emotionally I am still secretly entwined.

As we near Canterbury, our own Monte do Gozo moment comes on a B-road just outside the city. From here the sprawling gothic cathedral appears as a great cluster of spires and towers that shine near golden in the low afternoon light. First founded in the year 597, it's one of the oldest buildings in Christian England and, as such, is the seat of the Archbishop – the leader of the Church of England. Though it was ravaged by fire in 1174, suffered structural damage during an earthquake in 1382 and was desecrated during the Reformation, over time it has continuously been rebuilt, reconstructed and remodelled. It's a physical and palpable manifestation of devotion, and the sight of it makes me stop dead in my tracks. Others remark on its beauty as well as its imposing and strong walls. I agree that on the surface it does indeed look perfect, though I know all too well that a closer inspection will reveal the scars of a turbulent past.

At the cathedral we are allowed special access into the crypt. Here many pilgrims begin to pray and those who have been chatty throughout the last three days now fall into silent contemplation.

We hear that, once Becket was slain, some of the monks collected his blood – pre-empting his future sanctity. And how author and poet Geoffrey Chaucer, active during the height of pilgrimage here, captured some of the atmosphere felt in the crypt in his seminal *Canterbury Tales* – a collection of stories told by pilgrims in a contest for a free meal, en route to see this very shrine.

This spot would have been thronging back then, but in 1538 Henry VIII declared Becket a traitor and ordered his shrine to be destroyed. Worshipping icons was banned, pilgrimage prohibited. With no head of state ever officially rescinding his decree, what we have just done, I muse, is technically still forbidden. And something about this slightly clandestine act feels intoxicating.

Before I leave the cathedral I light a candle; not for Becket, but for myself. I know now that this walk is just the start for me – the first path of many. I am the singer who cannot sing and, somehow, I need to find my voice again.

TWO

Pilgrim's Progress

A broken trail marks the bright blue sky, as though scratched by a giant's fingernail. I gaze at it while lying on the grass in a graveyard, just outside Bedford in the small village of Elstow. As I watch, it begins to fray, and I know that soon it will disappear completely.

The sound of a squeaky wheel interrupts my musings on the vapour trails above and I sit up to see a caretaker wheeling old, dead flowers he's gathered from people's headstones over to a large compost heap in the corner. I nod at him; he doesn't return it. So I rest on the grass again, contemplating the path ahead as well as the one I've already trod to get me here.

'Are you okay?', asked a voice from somewhere above me.

Her words rang in my head for several seconds while I desperately tried to make sense of them. It had all happened so very quickly. One minute I'd been riding my bicycle downhill – as I did every night after working late at the office – enjoying that slightly thrilling but terrifying moment as I sped up and overtook the cars lined up waiting for the traffic lights.

That night was different, though. It was wet. It was windy. It was dark. I was tired. I was going to press with the magazine and left work even later than usual. The driver was in a hurry, couldn't bear to wait the extra few seconds it would take to pass me on a wider part of the road. Instead, he raced by, giving me hardly any space at all. The movement created an up-draught of wind, which caused me to wobble. I thought I had everything under control. I thought it would all be okay.

But as he sped off into the night I couldn't right myself. The handlebars shook violently in my grip. The brakes did nothing to slow me. I accepted my fate – all I could do was wait for impact.

It seemed to take forever to come. I remember flying over the handlebars. I remember thinking I should protect my head (I was, of course, wearing a helmet). I remember worrying about my laptop and my phone. It was like watching something happen in slow motion over several minutes – in reality it was just seconds.

At first I felt no pain at all. I lay there in shock, not really understanding what was happening. Then I heard the woman's concerned voice. I looked up to see the car speeding off, its tail-lights glowing red as it disappeared around the corner.

Another car was coming towards me. Now, lying in a heap on the road, I felt helpless. The vehicle seemed to be stopping but the driver had simply slowed down to swerve around me and carry on up the road. I felt like human roadkill. And I didn't feel like getting up at all. But her voice was calling me again ...

'Yes ...' I finally replied, not recognising the tiny sound that came out of my throat. Instinctively, I began to hoist myself up, and that's when the pain came. Fast.

All across my chest, with every single breath.

I somehow pulled myself up to standing, attempting to move off the road. Luckily (and unusually) no cars were behind me. I stumbled with the pain in my knees. My head was spinning, I felt sick, I saw only blotches.

The woman caught me in her arms, her son went to pick up my bike. I tried to tell them I'd be fine, to go about their evening, to leave me to it. I didn't want to admit how much pain I was in – I hated showing any sign of weakness to anyone. I was embarrassed it had happened at all. She wouldn't listen.

Instead, she did two things. The first – despite my protests – was to call an ambulance. Just as well, as due to the bruising and pain in my neck and back I would spend the next few hours strapped to a board with suspected spinal and neck injuries in a cold A&E department, eventually diagnosed with a suspected hairline fracture of my sternum as well as multiple cuts and bruises elsewhere. The second was what changed something in me.

She refused to leave, even when I told her to go.

The whole time, until they got me into the ambulance, she kept talking to me, kept letting me know someone was there who cared. She held on to me the entire time and put her arm around me. Normally I would try to shrug it off, but I had no energy. For once, I let somebody care.

And when she eventually did leave, she gave me a giant maternal hug and a kiss on the head and told me everything would be all right. It took all I had to stop from breaking down. At that moment, at that particular point, on that particular day, I needed to know that someone cared about what happened to me. That someone wanted me to be okay. That I mattered. And she did. I don't think she'll ever know how much it meant, and I'll never even know her name.

After my bike accident, I knew something had to change. My job was hard. The sale of the company was imminent and the small team ran like a dysfunctional family. In the absence of anything else I had allowed myself to become lost to it, to the point where I couldn't work out where my life ended and the job began. I dreaded going home. I would wake up at six in the morning, which crept gradually earlier, so eager was I to get into the office, to escape the uncomfortable thoughts and feelings that would ambush me without warning when I was back at my house. They came all the time: when I took a book off a shelf, reached for a particular glass in the cupboard, or stumbled upon a photo I thought I'd removed. Weekends were the worst. As Friday approached, I would desperately try to avoid going home, to a place where everything would be quiet and I would be left to my own dark thoughts.

On one particular Saturday evening I couldn't bear any part of my life any more. I felt as though I was trapped on a carousel, desperate to get off.

So I took two packets of sleeping pills and a bottle of whisky and went for a night hike into the woods nearby. I sat on a small hilltop and cried under the light of a story-book moon while the monotonous call of nightjars filled the increasing darkness.

And then my phone rang. It was someone I barely knew at all. She had recently been through a messy divorce; we'd met a couple of times and exchanged a few messages on social media. I'd happened to send her a supportive note once, which began a dialogue. But because she hadn't heard from me in a while she was concerned. She didn't have to say much to me that night, but she did convince me that no matter what I was feeling at that moment, taking my own life was not the answer.

The very next morning she convinced me to see a doctor, who diagnosed me with depression. She started me on a course of anti-depressants and urged me to talk to someone. And so I – reluctantly – started to see a therapist.

Nowadays everyone seems to be in therapy of some kind, but for me even the word when it was first uttered took me back to one morning when I was just thirteen. I'd heard a commotion downstairs, but when I tried to go into the living room my mum stopped me. My dad was very ill, she said, and the doctor was coming.

It wasn't like Dad ever to be ill. To him, sick days were something to be avoided at all costs – even as kids, unless we were truly at death's door, we were sent to school. Between Dad's staunch work ethic and my mum's job as a nurse, there was no feigning illness (though Mum sometimes took pity on me and would write me a note to get me out of gym, using her most inventive medical language:

'Phoebe cannot participate today as she has an upper respiratory tract infection, likely viral rhinitis.' Essentially, a common cold).

When the doctor came, I peered through the crack in the door as it shut behind him to see my dad lying on the settee covered with a crocheted blanket my mum had made. He didn't look poorly as such, just extremely tired. He was still in his pyjamas and it was nearly 10 am.

For days he was in bed as various euphemisms about his condition were bandied around. My granny, his mum, came to look after us so that my mum could go back to work, and would make comments on how he 'needed to pull himself together' and 'this didn't happen in my day'. Granny was the daughter of a single mum in the 1930s – her dad died when she was two, drowned at sea. She herself was widowed as a teenager, after which she became a sergeant in the Second World War. So it made sense that she didn't believe anyone could ever have things as bad as her generation.

Months went by and Dad didn't go back to work. He had slowly climbed his way up the ladder over the years, to become a manager of a loss-adjusting firm in our town. His job title always baffled my friends, but basically – I told them – when someone lost something he would go and work out how much it was worth and tell the insurance company what they should pay to the policyholder.

It was undoubtedly emotionally draining work – the pressure from the owner on one side, and, on the other, the nod-nod, wink-wink 'get us a good deal' of an insurance company trying to pay out as little as possible. If you were fair, as I believe my dad was, you were disliked by both parties.

I never really understood what his days entailed; all I knew was that his co-workers saw him a lot more than we did. He would go into the office on weekends and during school holidays, even in the weeks he'd taken off to look after me and my older brother, often leaving us waiting in the car outside, sometimes for hours. He'd take calls at home constantly, no matter what the time, and if a big event happened – like the time huge swathes of the North Wales coast got flooded – we wouldn't see him for weeks.

Suddenly, we saw Dad all the time, but he barely spoke. It was as though the dad I knew had gone somewhere and all that was left was his shadow, sitting in the chair in the living room, occasionally getting up to make a cup of tea. Finally, his illness was given a name: he'd had 'a nervous breakdown'.

I didn't understand what that meant, and now the term is no longer used as it isn't a proper medical diagnosis. But I did understand that work had caused him stress to the point of no return. His mind simply couldn't cope with the anxiety and constant crisis and pressure put on him from all sides and so it gave up, and his body followed.

After some time he tried going back to work, but his employer seemed keen for him to fail, making him relocate to another office, at a lower rank, with a commute that took hours each day. There he was made to see a psychiatrist. The way everyone talked about it, that was the most shameful outcome possible.

From that point on the idea of therapy was conflated in my mind as being the cause of problems rather than the solution.

Years later, sat in my own therapist's room, overlooking a perfectly manicured rectangular garden, I allowed myself to cry. I wept and wept, sometimes so uncontrollably I heard myself actually howl. When was the last time I'd done something just because I'd wanted to, she asked me. The only incident I could think of that came close to that had happened months earlier on The Old Way, but only by accident.

Perhaps I should try another pilgrimage, she suggested. And I agreed.

But this time I knew I wanted to be alone.

I had stumbled upon the John Bunyan Trail quite by accident, having a couple of weeks earlier arranged to meet a friend who lives in Peterborough. We agreed on a halfway point between us for lunch. That place turned out to be

Bedford. I arrived uncharacteristically early and set about finding an easy-to-spot meeting point. Without knowing it, I'd chosen to connect with her within metres of a statue of Bedford local John Bunyan, author of *The Pilgrim's Progress*.

Before then I knew little about the man. I recalled us struggling through the book in school, with its Old English language and thick allegorical themes. But I hadn't really appreciated quite how celebrated this work was until recently.

First published in 1676 – after pilgrimages were banned, of course – *The Pilgrim's Progress* has been continuously in print. It has been translated into around two hundred languages, in over a thousand editions – from picture books to bespoke children's versions, modern retellings for grown-ups, resources for teachers, not to mention cartoon adaptations, films and TV shows. Its influence can be found in the work of countless other authors, including C. S. Lewis, who went on to pen the religiously symbolic *The Lion, the Witch and the Wardrobe*; Charlotte Brontë, for whom Bunyan's tale helped inspire the trials and hardships of her heroine in *Jane Eyre*; and children's author Enid Blyton, who used it as inspiration for her religious text *The Land of Far-Beyond*.

And, in 1995, the book became the basis for another idea: a walk. To celebrate the diamond jubilee of the Ramblers Association (a British charity that works to protect pathways in the countryside to ensure walking is an activity open to all) the local Bedfordshire group decided to waymark and produce a guide to a route they called the John Bunyan Trail. The idea was that it would take in beautiful parts of the county, all with historical links to the local author, transposing the real places he would have frequented and doubtlessly been inspired by with those he plucked from his imagination and inserted into the pages of his tome. All this could be done succinctly over 131 kilometres.

Purposely setting out on another pilgrimage seemed strangely foreign. Would I still feel like a cheat, as I did back in Spain? I certainly didn't feel emotionally prepared, and I definitely didn't want to sign up for a group hike to be surrounded by hymns, candlelight and expectation. In fact, I wanted to do a walk that felt as little like an actual pilgrimage as possible. For a not-quite pilgrim like myself, and a writer, the Bunyan Trail seemed a good place to start.

The route begins by the statue of the man himself in Bedford city centre. Amid the coffeehouses and fast-food restaurants, discount clothes stores and vape shops, I follow the black-and-white signs that weave consistently between the modern and the ancient. At 17 St Cuthbert's Street a blue heritage plaque indicates the site where

Bunyan's former home stood. He lived here as an adult with his children and second wife (his first died shortly after they moved in). The path continues with a stop at a church, which sits alongside a pretty garden and fairly grand red-brick building that now houses a museum in his name. Inside stands a low-budget mannequin dressed up to look like Bunyan, along with artefacts from his life and pages from his will.

I try to read everything I can, to soak up as much as possible from this great storyteller's past, but the well-meaning volunteer wants to talk to me about my visit, so I spend most of the time nodding and moving past the belongings in a blur. I am led out of the building by waymarkers, over to the main high street and the outside of an ice-cream shop selling gelatos, themed in mono-chrome with a splash of deep red. Here, the plaque on the ground informs me, is the site of the Old Gaol – the place where Bunyan had been imprisoned in 1660 for preaching in the countryside, something that was forbidden. Back then, following the restoration of the monarchy (after a brief eleven-year period that saw Britain become a repub-lic) there was deep-seated paranoia that any religious meeting was actually cover for a planned Royal assassina-tion plot, so arrest was the usual outcome. Bunyan would remain in the gaol for twelve years, unrepentant, while inside its cold walls he penned his most famous work about Christian, an everyman, who leaves his old life and family in the City of Destruction, bound for redemption in the Celestial City.

The use of an 'everyman' is a particular narrative technique, employed by a writer to make the readers identify with a character and take on their perspective easily. To work, this character has to be fairly unremarkable, bland even, so that anyone can identify with them. Reading *Pilgrim's Progress* as an adult I really resented Christian. Something about him grated. He seemed too willing to go along with things and was hypercritical of people who disagreed with him. Perhaps he reminded me of something I'd become.

Following in Bunyan's footsteps I leave the city and head south, from the place where his everyman was created to the village of Elstow – the place where the author himself was born.

Along the way I meander beside the River Ouse, coming to the site where he was baptised in these waters. There is a bitterness in the air, so cold it makes my lips sting. But the sky is clear and the sun is out. The water looks perilously inviting.

The village of Elstow is picturesque and quiet, centred around a stone abbey that once housed an order of Benedictine nuns. Here, Bunyan enjoyed a well-documented love of dancing, bell-ringing (the fifth bell in the tower of the abbey is still known as 'Bunyan's Bell') and singing too. As he got older, he worried that all the pleasures he had enjoyed were actually sins. Without anyone seemingly telling him not to do the things he loved, or even seeing a reason not to do these things, Bunyan began to withdraw from his passions and took a different road from his friends. I can't decide whether that makes him strong or weak. But it does sound remarkably familiar.

I try to gain access to the inside of the abbey, which sits across a pretty green from the orange-bricked, timber-framed building of Moot Hall (in its time a marketplace, meeting room, educational centre, a site for country fairs and now home to Bunyan memorabilia), but it is locked. So I find myself lying on the grass and looking up at the sky. I feel as far from the City of Destruction as is possible.

It's difficult to know what a route has to encompass to be classed as a pilgrimage rather than simply a walk. On the Camino the authorities say it needs to be a set distance. When I ask the staff at the John Bunyan Museum they say they believe it has to be a walk with a purpose. The British Pilgrim Trust maintain it has nothing to do with religion, although all their routes feature churches or holy places. And, reading Bunyan's book, where his everyman embarks on a journey to heaven carrying a huge – literal – burden on his back, it would seem that to be a true pilgrimage, there has to be some degree of difficulty involved in it.

I hadn't yet decided if I was a pilgrim. But I leave the village carrying my own invisible burden still.

'It seems to me,' said the therapist as I apologised to her for using up yet another box of tissues, 'that you have a habit of doing things out of a sense of duty for others, to help them, but never ask anyone to help you.'

We had spent the last two sessions talking about my sense of guilt, particularly at having ended relationships, so her assertion made me pause.

I thought back to what we'd just been discussing minutes before to try and work out what she was getting at. The last thing I could remember I'd mentioned was losing my mum.

But we'd gone further back than that, to the time when I'd had a young and furious fling. Mum found out I'd stayed at my boyfriend's house and said that if I did it again, I would be forced to move out of the family home. I tried to reason with her, and then again with my dad. Why were there different rules for my brother and I? We were different, I was told. He was a boy, I was a girl. I could get pregnant, he could not. I learned then that as a woman, I would be bound to a different set of rules and expectations. I was to be compliant. If not, the consequence was rejection.

My mother and I were both equally stubborn; I couldn't be seen to back down.

So I left, as you do at seventeen, in a storm of foul language and curses. I didn't want to leave home. I loved my room. It was my sanctuary, my space to retreat to whenever things got too much. It had seen me through Dad's breakdown, allowed me space when friendships faltered or boyfriends came and went, and now it was to be taken away from me. When I returned several days later, my brother had already been moved into my bedroom and all I could do was take some belongings and leave again.

'Mum had her reasons,' I said to my counsellor defiantly; 'they both did.'

'You don't need to make excuses for them,' she said. 'It's okay that you felt abandoned.'

After leaving home I found myself moving from place to place trying to carve out a space where I felt I belonged. I slept on couches, shared single beds and dreamed of the day I could afford to get my own safe space.

When Mum got sick a couple of years later, and time and space had slowly begun to heal our rift, her prognosis came back much worse than expected. The cancer had spread and I wasn't there to help. Now I felt I was the one who had done the abandoning.

I returned home one day to find her on the settee after what would turn out to be a failed surgery to remove the tumour. She'd been sick on the floor after attempting to eat an apple and drink some blueberry juice – she now demanded so-called superfoods for every meal – but she couldn't get up because she felt so dizzy.

As a child my mum had primarily been the one to look after us when we got sick, so the sight of her sat helpless, surrounded by her own purple vomit, made me want to scream in anguish. I stood there for a few seconds, remembering the time I arrived home aged fifteen, drunk but trying to act sober, and proceeded to throw up on her shoes in the hallway, just steps from where I now stood.

'Don't worry,' I told her, 'I'll clean it up.'

When Christian made a decision to leave behind his old life in the City of Destruction he couldn't persuade anyone to go with him. Some tried, but when things got difficult – such as in the Slough of Despond, the water that is today usually equated with Elstow Brook alongside which I now wander – they left him to it.

Before I lost Mum I lived a very different life. I was a walking cliché. I would dance and sing like there was no tomorrow. Life was an unending ribbon of opportunity, and if I occasionally missed one it didn't matter, because another would come streaming out to replace it.

I knew her death was coming the moment I woke up one late August morning in a bed that wasn't mine. I looked out of the window at the dappled light from the sun just breaking through a band of thick cloud, and I could almost hear her voice whisper among the raucous calls of herring gulls, 'This is a good day to die.'

Just a few days previously I'd found myself back in the seaside town of Rhyl. I'd been in the USA taking a summer job in my break from university, working in a supermarket in perhaps the most unglamorous state in the entire country: Delaware.

There I operated the checkout, surrounded by co-workers called Glen, Dale and Elaine, and those known by their surnames only, like Hudson and White. Most lived in trailers, and I lived in a tiny house with no air conditioning in the owner's back garden.

Before I'd headed out there I'd gone to see my mum in the cancer unit, a new building they'd finished not long before she needed it, full of the smell of fresh paint and new computers almost singing with the promise that good things can only happen there.

'I'm not going to go,' I told her as I handed over the pair of scissors that she'd asked me to bring in. She was starting radiotherapy the next day to try and shrink the cancer that had now metastasised to her brain, and the hairdressers on the ward had cancelled her appointment last minute. I'd thought I could go in and cut it for her, but when I arrived we both knew that was impossible, for either of us.

'I won't let you stay,' she replied. 'You have to go. Do you get it? You have to go for me. Don't get stuck where you don't want to be. Get out while you can. I didn't and it's too late for me, but it's not for you.'

Those words followed me when I left and got on a flight to New York. I was so ill with worry that I vomited at the airport, again in the toilet of the plane and once more when I took the Greyhound bus to Bethany Beach. I went to sleep the first night and hoped I'd wake up back home again.

Weeks passed and we wrote each other letters. She made jokes at first, and told me at length about her wig and her activities on the wards, trying yoga and various crafts. But over time the notes became shorter and the humour was gone. The last time I spoke to her on the phone she told me I was her ray of sunshine when everything else got too dark.

On what was to be my last day at the supermarket – though I didn't know it at the time – White came up to me on my break in the parking lot with a crate covered in cloth. He tried to scare me by revealing a set of pincers from a crab and chasing me with them. I didn't move.

'Why aren't you scared?' he'd asked.

That phrase rung in my head hours later, at 5.35 am, when the phone next to my bed rang loud and shrill. It was an old rotary dial and sounded like a fire alarm ringing with intense ferocity. Even before I picked it up I knew what was coming.

'You've got to come home,' said my dad's voice, assertive, unwavering. 'You've got to come home, now.'

The cry that came out of my mouth that morning was one I've not heard before or since. It was more animal than human, a note of anguish on a scale reserved for wild creatures, not civilised people. The next few hours passed in a blur of shaky phone conversations with airlines and desperate pleas with the Greyhound bus office to let me switch dates on my ticket.

On the plane back, less than twenty-four hours later, I didn't sleep a single second. At that point in my life I was a particularly nervous flier, but on that day I didn't care if we crashed. My whole world was about to go up in smoke. As I watched the sunset, one of the most vivid I'd seen in my life, I felt an odd sense of calm.

I went straight to see her and cried at her feet while she struggled to say even a few words to me. She was grappling with both pain and morphine, managing to just whisper: 'I always miss you when you're not with me.'

When I arrived at the hospice on her last day with us, I once more felt a strange sense of peace. The nurse who let me in was unhurried and led me slowly to her room. Around her stood several other nurses and, next to them, my dad.

'I think she's gone,' he said.

But he was wrong. She sat up for a second, streams of thick yellow liquid pouring from her mouth. The so-called terminal secretions, where a body can no longer swallow accumulating saliva and so it gathers at the back of the throat and on the lungs. I remember when she had one of her earlier surgeries and Dad and my brother said she waved at them when she was being put to sleep. When she came to, she said she wasn't waving, she was actually calling for help. She felt like she was the subject of that poem I had studied in school by Stevie Smith, 'Not Waving but Drowning'.

I ran around the bed to stand by her side and pushed a nurse out of the way so I could take her hand in mine.

'I'm here, Mum,' I said as she fought for air; 'we're all here and we love you.'

She didn't try to take another breath after that.

Following the funeral, Dad urged me to go back to my studies. I was the first one in the family to get into university and he was adamant that Mum would have wanted me to carry on. And I did go back, though I knew it wasn't the same. I could no longer laugh as easily or take life quite so lightly. I had looked death head on and seen my mother's face looking back. I had been presented with my own mortality, and so young.

None of my friends knew loss. Their conversations now seemed pointless. They talked to me carefully as though worried I would break, until they simply stopped talking to me at all. It was as if hanging out with me would infect them with the same thing – whatever it was – that was taking hold of me. And so they left me on my own, and I told myself I was all the better for it.

On my second day on the Bunyan Trail I reach All Saints' Church. It sits at the top of a chalk hill in Shillington, a small village on the border with Hertfordshire. Much of the walking until this point had been on tracks and roads, with the sporadic field that had once been muddy, but in the frosty air had solidified to form crests and waves amid patches of dying grass. Now, from this height, the view over the surrounding countryside stretched on in a glorious crumpled blanket of yellows, browns and greens. I am not interested in many of the churches I pass, but this one, with its door resembling a sunbeam, piques my interest.

Called the Cathedral of the Chilterns – themselves thought to be Bunyan's 'Delectable Mountains', from which Christian first spies the Celestial City – I choose it as the place to take a minute and simply rest.

A pair of red kites swoop above me, whistling to one another as they fly. Ornithologists say they do it to signal a threat to the nest or, conversely, just because they are having a good time. I wish I could decode its meaning.

Over the next three days I walk and camp along the route, making my way on this circular pathway, back to the beginning. By day I try to match Bunyan's descriptions of landmarks with those I can see on the trail, and at night I make notes of my discoveries.

My highlight comes as I near Sharpenhoe Clappers, a spur of ground that rises from an otherwise flat landscape of arable farmland, which I had spied from the cowslip-lined edges of Barton Hills earlier that morning. The name 'clappers' points to an ancient network of rabbit warrens that would once have been important to people as a source of food and fur. The journey to the summit from the south is unremarkable, but as I near the edge the views of the land make me stop and hold my breath. I had never before appreciated that swathes of rolling chalkland could be quite so dramatic – and full of wildlife. Orange-tipped butterflies land on nettle leaves as I edge through pockets of foliage. Green woodpeckers hungrily tap at the beech trees and colonies of dog's mercury festoon the woodland floor.

I tuck my bivvy bag in the long grass near a cluster of beech trees where lovers from the 1960s and 70s have carved their names and the dates into the bark. I lie on top of my sleeping bag for what feels like minutes, watching the darkness of the leaves begin to merge with the darkening fragments of light as dusk falls and is replaced by night. Some people are scared of walking in the dark, but more than a decade of choosing to purposely head out into it makes me yearn for it when I am within the confines of four walls. Sleep comes to me more easily in these woods than it has over the nights before, as though I have left something I've been carrying at the bottom of that hill.

I wake early, surrounded by a thick shroud of cloud, evoking the ghost of the Celtic chieftain Cassivellaunus, who led a charge against Julius Caesar in 54 BC and is said to haunt this forest. The route onwards passes by an old oak tree in which Bunyan preached, using its hollowed trunk as a pulpit. I can even make out the footholds on which he might have stood shouting his sermons. Despite my own aversion to churchgoing, I love the way that, faced with being unable to preach in a church without a licence, Bunyan used the outdoors and nature as his lectern. I stand in the field, on top of his tree, while a recently planted copse of silver birch trees seems to offer a round of applause, as their leaves rustle in the wind.

In the years I've been without her, I have tended to feel my mum's presence most keenly at the top of mountains.

It's not that she was an ardent fan of high places, in fact to my knowledge she never climbed any. But it is, inexplicably, when I'm in those places that I can feel her hand on the back of my head. The summits of our landscapes have almost become the place where I commune with my own mother.

In *The Pilgrim's Progress*, among the many challenges Christian faces are geographical sites with foreboding names like the 'Valley of the Shadow of Death', said to be a gorge in Millbrook; Doubting Castle, purportedly Ampthill Castle (now just fields topped with a beacon); and the Hill of Difficulty, allegedly the steepest point along the B530 road to Bedford. Until this point I have been like that early bishop in Sardis, looking for the physical landmarks in order to somehow make the imaginary true. But somewhere after the latter I stop trying to match up the real places with Bunyan's fictional ones and allow myself time to simply enjoy the walk.

I gaze in wonder at Houghton House, the Grade I listed seventeenth-century ruined mansion, stripped and sold for parts in 1794. I pick bushels of wild crab-apples, vowing to take them home and make jam from scratch. And I try to peer over the fences of Millbrook Proving Ground where car manufacturers take their top-secret inventions to test them on a variety of tracks. Indulging my whims in this way was perhaps my own version of Christian's Vanity Fair –

distracted by the fanciful, delaying me reaching my goal. I decide I would never have made it to the Celestial City.

On my final day, arriving in Bromham, seventeen kilometres from the end, I begin to look at Bunyan's links to the real-life places again. Here at the edge of the village is a church where it's said he once preached. I follow the path to pass a holy well, a spring that local legend says never freezes and never dries up. Around it a stone arch has been constructed, making it glow almost pallid white amid the darkness caused by the canopy of trees that surround it. Despite its unnatural colour, moss is already building up along the edges of the waterline and Christ's Hair ferns penetrate through nearly every seam in the mortar. It won't be long before nature reclaims this spring.

Inside its arches two women are filling empty bottles with water and they offer me some to try.

'Purest you'll ever drink,' one assures me. 'I get all my family's water from here.'

I take the bottle from her; the liquid inside is ice cold on my tongue and tastes almost like milk as it drips down my throat. This well may have been the place where, when Christian finally sheds the burden from his back, it rolls down a slope to land in a manmade sepulchre.

As I make my way slowly back to a waiting train, under the dim glow of twilight, I wonder if any of my burdens will ever be laid to rest as his was. I had spent the last week reading about how Christian – and through him Bunyan – had battled with Sloth and Presumption, taken on Formality and Hypocrisy, and outsmarted The Flatterer and Mistrust. But it wasn't his story I needed to read if I was to remove my burden and reach my own Celestial City.

Bunyan had used his book to write his way out of an actual prison, through imagination, and though I wasn't behind bars in the physical sense, mentally I still felt as though I was trapped in a cell of my own making.

As I climbed aboard the train that night, leaving the City of Destruction behind, I knew I must start a chain of events in motion to begin my own personal quest for deliverance.

THREE

Lost

My fingers tremble uncontrollably. With each bleep of the ringtone I hold my breath.

Finally, he answers.

'Dad?' I say, in a small voice. 'I'm coming home.'

I always experience a heady concoction of emotions when faced with going back to the setting of my childhood, especially after years of being away. In some ways it brings with it a wave of nostalgia and great comfort. In others it makes me feel like I have failed at growing up, that the goal I once set in defiance of my parents has not been properly reached. I am going backwards when I should be moving forwards.

After Mum died, Dad sold the family home and moved to a town on the side of a motorway, coincidentally near to the cancer ward and hospice where she spent her final weeks alive and, handily, much closer to a woman he was becoming involved with.

The old family home had been a living, breathing version of my mum. Having grown up in Derbyshire with so little, having baths in an old tin trough in front of the fire, walking out in the cold night air to use a toilet, and never having any personal trinkets in her tiny two-up, two-down terrace, she had been adamant that our house would be filled with 'things'. Mum never really travelled abroad. She was too scared of planes, and the one time she went by ferry to France she was severely seasick. But she loved to read about other countries. Every room in the house, including the bathroom, was stocked with books. From reams of fictional accounts of places near and far, to memoirs, travelogues and photography books so big that no shelf could hold them.

Some nights, when I was small, she'd take out one of these great volumes and show me pictures of the Moai in Easter Island, the wildebeest migration in Africa or the colourful temples of South East Asia.

Of all the countries she took me to through these pages, it was India that captured her imagination the most. Rather than family heirlooms or photos, the ornaments in our house were wooden elephants. Statues of Shiva and Ganesh danced on tables draped in sari fabrics; bracelets adorned with bells and charms looped around table lamps; and fabric laced with tiny mirrors hung from the walls and made the living room sparkle and dance with light when the sun came out, as though we were in a disco hall.

Our walls weren't magnolia, they were burnt orange or amaranth purple. Going into our living room was akin to walking through a series of bric-à-brac stalls in Delhi's Sarojini Nagar market.

At home you'd often hear Mum approaching long before she entered a room. She wore patchwork harem pants – before they were fashionable – and strings of bangles and anklets that jangled when she walked. Dad would dread her coming home from town, and especially after she'd visited a store that he – and therefore all of us – affectionately called 'the junk shop', for fear of what she might bring with her. The most hysterical purchase to me and my brother was a giant paper lampshade, so big that when she hung it no one could see the television.

As a little kid I didn't think anything of it. To me, my home was normal. It was only when I started going to friends' houses and met their mums – who wore neat two-pieces or jeans and t-shirts with denim jackets and shoulder pads, elegant jewellery that made no sound, and whose houses were immaculately clean and tidy with very little colour – that I got the sense that my mum was different. And so was I. Where other girls would covet dainty gifts made of gold for birthdays, I would ask for books full of words and photographs that could transport me to another place.

For the couple of weeks preceding Mum's funeral, I'd stayed at the family home with Dad so I could help organise everything. I'd slept on the sofa in the living room, where Mum had spent the last weeks before the pain became so bad that she had to be moved into a hospice for around-the-clock care. Despite it being a couple of years since I'd called this house my home, it still felt like the closest place I had to one. Surrounded by the familiar objects from my childhood, even though Mum was gone, the essence of her still lingered. When I lay on the settee, her trademark scent of Olbas oil (a blend of herbs and essential oils including peppermint, eucalyptus and wintergreen), which she'd apply to her pillow in eye-watering quantities, would permeate into the air for several seconds and for a moment I would forget she had gone at all.

In the month that passed after her cremation, I had to go back to university – on her dying insistence – but I would try and visit Dad often to check he was okay. The woman he had already started seeing was helping him 'sort the house'.

I knew it had to be done, but watching Mum being seemingly surgically removed from her home felt like a betrayal. I stopped going back and, in the end, when Dad sold the house and moved away, I felt relieved that I didn't have to see the place devoid of her. In my mind at least her presence would still remain intact.

Dad's new house is a single-storey dwelling that suits him well. Without my mum's influence there is not much colour, though it makes me smile when I see flourishes of her have not been completely erased – such as the brightly painted elephant table that sits alongside his new beige sofa.

By now, I'd worked my last day at the magazine. I handed in my notice a day after completing the John Bunyan Trail, and left a couple of months later in a hurricane of hugs, well wishes and more than a little envy. I had plans, ambitions, assignments, freedom – but with that came time and space to sit in my one-bedroom house and berate myself for being the person I was.

The time feels right, in some ways, to return to Wales, but I still feel apprehensive as I sit on the train from London bound for Flint, the carriage rocking me like a mother soothing her distressed child. Outside, the urban has already begun to relent to open countryside. That sight would have once made me silently rejoice, but now I just feel numb.

After my revelations in Bedford I began to look more seriously at the network of pilgrim paths that extend across the British Isles. I was astonished to learn just how many there were. From short day-long journeys between churches, to multi-day ancient routes following spiritual ley lines and border crossings, there were so many more to choose from than I ever anticipated. I stopped counting how many after I hit one hundred.

What surprised me most was just how many new ones had appeared only in the previous decade. It seemed that for reasons I couldn't yet fathom, a lot more people were headed out on 'journeys with purpose'.

Taking a leaf out of Bunyan's book I had decided that I wanted to walk somewhere for longer than a few days. Time was now on my side, so a couple of weeks was more than possible and a welcome distraction.

I'd considered many routes that fit the bill: the St Wilfrid's Way, which follows in the footsteps of the somewhat controversial eponymous seventh-century saint (he had a penchant for living the high life and was banished twice from Northumbria), that starts in the north of England, at Hexham Abbey, and continues up the country before ending, after a journey over the Cheviots and through the Scottish borders, at the church of St Mary's in Edinburgh. At 240 kilometres that one would take me just over two weeks.

Or there was the Cornish Celtic Way, launched in 2017. A 201-kilometre stroll that would see me cross the peninsula in the far south-west corner of England twice as I combined the Saints' Way with the St Michael's Way, visiting holy wells and spiritual sites. On this one I could even get a passport and collect stamps in true Camino style.

Both sounded beautiful and worthy of my time. But then I stumbled across the Taith Pererin Gogledd Cymru, aka the North Wales Pilgrim's Way.

The trail was officially launched in 2015, the year before I walked Spain's Camino. The designation may be new, but it follows an ancient route taken by medieval pilgrims bound for Bardsey Island from the Dee Valley back in the sixth century. At over 225 kilometres, it promised to take me across the rivers and mountains of Snowdonia, along the coast where I grew up, through villages where I holidayed with Mum, and to beaches where I went rock pooling with my brother. It was as though someone had plotted points from my childhood and mapped them in a spiritual quest just for me. Once I knew it existed, I could take on no other path before this one was done. And so I packed my bag and boarded the train, resolutely bound north.

When I first told Dad I was getting help for my mental health I was scared. From a young age I feel I've been conditioned to care for others before myself – as a young girl I was praised for being 'caring, kind and loving', whereas my brother was complimented for being 'brave and strong'.

It seems that nearly every woman is – often silently – assigned the role of 'dutiful daughter', made to feel responsible for everyone else, making sure that they are okay, even at the expense of their own happiness and needs. And in a way, my own mum asked this of me before she died. On her last Mother's Day she told me that if something did happen to her she wouldn't worry about me as she knew I would be all right, but she did have concerns about my brother and Dad. She asked me to look out for them to make sure they were happy. Without hesitation I agreed. On the surface I don't look like a dutiful daughter, I'm sure. I left home very young, I went to America when my mum got really sick, and now I am living far from what remains of my family. But the guilt and sense of duty to check that everyone is happy, to refrain from sharing my problems, is real.

The woman Dad started a relationship with shortly after Mum died seemed to hate me. If I went to see him she would ask probing questions, as though getting at a lack of integrity and intelligence in me. If I went to his place between semesters for a few days and he was at work, she would appear, unannounced, and pretend she could 'smell something funny', implying I had been smoking weed or worse. She would refer to me as 'that girl' to my granny and seemed to stir my dad into nit-picking about things I did or said.

There was a single moment when it all came to a head. When I cracked and broke character. My brother and I had planned a meal with Dad, but when he arrived home he was desperate to get out of it and go and see her instead. I thought I could remain calm, but I snapped and shouted and screamed at him about his priorities and how quickly he had seemed to get into bed with her after we lost my mum. He left the house, and I knew then that if he was made to choose between me and her, it would never be me who won.

And so I stopped trying to fight it. I let her comments slide. I smiled and nodded. I went through the motions of pretending I was unaffected. I made her believe we were friends. It was hard. Especially when she made disparaging comments about how my mum used to be or look. And it really hurt when I saw that the patchwork quilt Mum had bought me as a child had somehow ended up in this woman's house, on the bed in her spare room. Still, I did not cry. After all, I'd already lost one parent; there was no way I was going to lose another to her.

While this was happening, I noticed this sense that I must please others at the expense of myself shifting to other relationships and friendships too. I wasn't feisty any more. I didn't protest and argue when I felt I was in the right. I tried, to all intents and purposes, to sink into the scenery, as though I was as bland as magnolia wallpaper.

My granny – my dad's mum, a person who had struggled to connect with me since I was a teenager (telling me she preferred boys as they were less complicated) – became an unexpected ally. She had become less physically able to clean and wash in the years since Mum passed and Dad's partner's control over her was even worse. We would write to each other in secret about 'that woman', then destroy the evidence lest we should be caught and punished. Gradually, the photographs Granny had of me on her sideboard were moved out of her view, before disappearing completely. Yet we both accepted it as martyrs, believing we were somehow doing it for the greater good, to enable my dad to be as happy as he could be after losing his wife. My brother, meanwhile, seemed to escape this new woman's disdain; I'm unsure whether or not this was down to his gender.

When Granny died too, a few years later, in a cold empty room with white walls devoid of personal effects, I felt that another piece of me was cremated with her.

By the time I went on anti-depressants myself, Dad had long been off his. It was one of the first things he did when Mum died, on the advice of that woman. He said it was because he couldn't cry.

That was not my experience on medication. Tears would sometimes come unexpectedly in inappropriate moments – on a flight to Nepal in the middle of an innocuous conversation with another passenger, or mid-way through an interview I was recording for a radio programme. I learned to keep tissues with me and feign hay fever to disguise it. I never wanted my discomfort to make others feel bad. As though my tears could somehow destroy someone's perception of a woman who had it all together.

It was only a while after Dad and that woman had parted ways that I revealed details of my medication to him. I was surprised by the warmth and love he showed me. It floored me.

At first it felt like a trick, as if, were I to let my guard down, I would open myself up to feel the cold hard shove of rejection almost immediately. Since he'd ignored my pleas when I didn't want to leave home, taken his partner's side consistently over mine when we lost Mum, and even told my brother he wanted me to stop calling him as often as I was doing, as he felt like I was 'checking up on him', the risk of him abandoning me again was palpable. I told my therapist I didn't believe him, that I was convinced his offer to help wasn't real or, at least, was born of guilt.

'Let him help,' she said. 'It doesn't matter the reason it's offered. You need to start letting people in. You cannot do this all on your own.'

The North Wales Pilgrim's Way begins in Holywell, Flintshire, at the ruins of Basingwerk Abbey, a place that in medieval times served as a hospital, treating pilgrims on their way to Bardsey Island.

It seems an apt beginning on a route that is supposed to heal me.

I walk through the old arches of the abbey – built first in 1131 and then remodelled in the thirteenth century – where families were out having picnics in the unseasonably warm weather. The benches where Cistercian monks would sit and read still remain. Alongside them, I pass the former parlour – the one place in the complex where the monks were permitted to break their silence and speak. There was no one there for me to utter a word to.

Allowing myself to be swept up in the sense of doing my first 'proper' Camino, I head to the shop where an assistant called David sells me a Pasbort Y Pererin, my pilgrim passport, for a pound, and gives me my first stamp in wet black ink. I ask him how many people he has seen walking the trail and he says between one and two hundred in a season, which runs between April and August.

'I don't suppose many will be walking it now,' he says as he hands over the slim booklet. Emblazoned on the cover is the photograph of my destination, Bardsey, dappled in light from an overcast sky. 'Walk safe,' he tells me.

I am pleased. I purposely came early in the year to avoid crowds of any kind. I thank him and leave, the interaction rubber-stamping the start, as though I'd signed an obligation that I must now fulfil.

The beginning of any multi-day walk is filled with a strange kind of anticipation. Everything seems slightly novel and new. After months in the city, the trees that arch over the pathway as I pass the site of former flour and cotton mills seem exceptionally green – almost to excess.

The first landmark I reach is St Winefride's Well, the place from which the nearby town of Holywell or Treffynnon (town of the well) gets its name. Winefride, or *Gwenffrewi*, who lived in the seventh century, was said to be the daughter of a local Welsh prince called Tweyth, and niece of the priest who served at St Bueno, a site now lost to festoons of ivy on a hill mere metres away from St Winefride's. It's said that a chief from Hawarden, known as Caradoc, tried to seduce her but, determined to remain chaste, this beautiful virgin ran towards the church to be saved by her uncle. She was ruthlessly pursued in her escape and before she could reach salvation was unceremoniously beheaded by her would-be suitor. However, where her now-detached cranium came to rest, a spring of water emerged from the ground and her uncle – finally arrived – placed her head back on her body and prayed. She miraculously came back to life and her murderer was swallowed into the ground.

This young woman saw out the next twenty-two years of her life as a nun, identifiable by a single white scar which encircled her neck, and was eventually elected to lead her convent as abbess (or Mother Superior). Though the site where this is alleged to have happened is named in her honour, she was never formally canonised as a saint despite living beatifically.

Throughout the year there are times when you can bathe in the water that comes from the same spring that ostensibly brought her back to life. I arrive too early to sample its healing properties so instead wander around the edge of its turquoise-tinged waters, watch candles flicker on the altar, and admire the Romanesque arches that rise above the encircled pool.

As I leave through the small museum, I spy a cluster of wooden staffs left behind by pilgrims who have made the journey here, arranged into an art installation. I wonder for a second if I should perhaps have brought my own.

The way from the well climbs steadily uphill. I begin to feel the first beads of perspiration blossom on my forehead as I rise to a high open field amid piping calls from the meadow pipits that flutter in front of me without warning, emerging from the long grass in jerky flocks. I stop at a high point where the views along the coast finally open up. I can see as far as the beaches of Talacre, where the white-washed, defunct lighthouse was a point where we once dared each other to reach as children trying to beat the incoming tide. The rectangular peninsula of The Wirral, a place whose residents are often known as 'woolly backs', sits opposite. They are not quite considered English, though they are not technically Welsh either.

Whenever I am at my home in the south-east of England, people say I speak too fast. I'm always being accused of being from somewhere 'north'. When I once went to narrate a story I'd written for BBC Radio 4, I was told by the editor how refreshing it was to hear someone 'more common' reading it. When I mention growing up in North Wales, people start to claim they can hear a Welsh twang in my voice, despite the coastal North Walian accent sounding like a mixture of Mancunian and Liverpudlian rather than anything approaching the elongated and stressed vowels you'd hear in the stereotypical Cardiff accent associated with the country. Yet when I return to the place I grew up, to them I sound 'English'. The Welsh I learned at school has been relegated to reading only and I am corrected constantly on place names that I know I am pronouncing as I always have.

The truth is – like the woolly backs – I am neither Welsh nor English. Born in Warrington, the first crossing point on the River Mersey and equidistant between the rival cities of Liverpool and Manchester, in a hospital on the idyllic-sounding Lovely Lane, I am, by government-issued documentation, English. Yet I don't really think I can claim it.

I could barely talk when we moved to Wales. I went to an Ysgol rather than a school, I greeted people with 'bore da', as much as 'hello', and thanked grown-ups with a polite 'diolch yn fawr'. I dutifully rolled my Rs, pronounced my double Ls with a lateral fricative tongue technique, and reminded others that a double 'd' should always be pronounced as 'th'.

Yet I knew I wasn't Welsh.

In the early years of primary school, we did a project on our families, and I was outed – without realising it – by my Cheshire-headed birth certificate and revelation that my parents were from Derbyshire and Kent. Some girls would make fun of me, telling me I must – stressed as a fact rather than a choice – support England rather than Wales in rugby or football. But Wales was the home I knew for the longest time, until I left it.

With Mum gone and the family house I'd grown up in sold, I feel I no longer have a base in the country I know best. Yet when I'm outside in the hills above the former county of Clwyd, looking down at the sea towards England or over to the mountains of Snowdonia, I get a tremendous rush of belonging.

On my pilgrimage I am surprised by the clarity with which I can see the peaks in the far distance. They appear as a blurred wave in pewter grey against a faint blue sky, and it's hard to fathom that even when I reach them I will only be at the midway point of my journey.

I continue on to Pantasaph, home of the former St Clare's Convent, once an orphanage for children left without family. When I lived in Wales it was abandoned to fall into disrepair, a ruin that we'd sometimes pass on the motorway, left charred from a fire. I would scare myself with made-up stories of ghosts within its old stone walls – the spirits of angry nuns and children who died too young. But in recent years it's been renovated and now sits as a cluster of luxury homes and apartments.

The church of St David is still standing alongside a former Franciscan retreat, which when I pass it, is permanently closed to the public; in 2022 it was reopened by a Vincentian Congregation and began to host people once more. Outside are elaborately carved Celtic crosses overhung by draping elder trees. I trace their intricate knots with my fingertips.

The guidebook I clutch tries to direct me to the beacon on top of Coed y Garreg, and point me to the Viking-influenced Maen Achwyfan cross, a tenth-century 10.5-metre-tall Christian relic hewn from a single piece of stone. Yet I have begun to spy landmarks from my past that are far more captivating and pull my attention from the present.

Wandering alongside the Animal Rescue Centre I recall being here many years before, when I was just nine. It was here we adopted our overfed tabby cat whose owner had just died. He came to us with the name Foxy, but Mum immediately changed it to Bilbo Baggins, a name he answered to without resistance. For the years we had him, alongside the two younger cats we'd nurtured from kittens, he seemed to live with a determination to do as little as possible. His back legs were so large they wobbled together when he walked. If you let him into the garden, as we did when Mum first brought him home, he proceeded to find a dry spot under our old slide and wait, patiently, until we let him back inside. He never explored beyond the back yard.

However, after our other two cats died in quick succession – the victim of cars rushing past too quickly on the road that ran behind our house – he changed. He started disappearing for hours and even days at a time. He came back with blood on his ear once, and another time, when I walked into town with my friend, we found him a good half-hour away and he followed us back home.

The death of his companions changed Bilbo Baggins and ultimately led him to the same fate – a run-in with a vehicle, seconds from the safety of our garden.

Soon after I pass the animal centre I reach the village of Llanasa, where I realise I've run out of water. I spot an old 'Parish Pump' and try my luck in case it still works. It doesn't. The church I had relied on to be open is shut and the pub – my Plan B – is also padlocked.

I start to move on, resigned to feeling parched. By now I have walked more than fifteen kilometres and, with my skinny frame, I'm growing tired and weak. A voice in my head tells me to knock on a door and ask for a drink. I try to ignore it, but then I see a couple arriving home at one of the huge houses on the main road. And for the first time on this trail I ask for help. The water tastes divine.

I make the decision to ascend Y Gop, a 251-metre manmade mound, thought to have been constructed during the end of the Stone Age. It's the second largest of its kind in Britain, after the celebrated Silbury Hill in Wiltshire, which receives many thousands of visitors each year on their circuit of monuments from the end of the Neolithic era – including nearby Stonehenge, West Kennet Long Barrow and Avebury Stone Circle.

This high hill, by comparison, sees hardly any visitors. Made of a jumble of local limestone and overlooking the village of Trelawnyd to the south, it was excavated just once back in 1886 by geologist and archaeologist Boyd Dawkins, who was disappointed to find only flint arrowheads and no burial chambers. Further down the slopes though, below the mysterious mini mountain, he found a cave. Now marked on the Ordnance Survey map, its entrance when he discovered it was choked with fallen stones and hand-placed rocks. It contained sediment from the last Ice Age as well as the remains of hyenas, bison and reindeer – the latter showing bite marks from the former. Further in, skeletal remains of humans were recovered from walled chambers, probably a family group, positioned as though hunched together in a secret meeting.

I stand on the very top of the hillside thinking about the hidden secrets that may still remain beneath my feet. I look over to the north where the hill of Gwaenysgor – or 'Gwhiny' hill as we called it in school – rises above the seaside town of Prestatyn.

After Mum died, I travelled a lot. I found countries where I could attain working visas – the USA, Canada, Australia – and then filled in the gaps between with bargain flights that took me to South Africa, Asia and the Pacific Islands. It was as though, in the years immediately after her death, I tried to cram in the lifetime of travel she wanted but never managed to achieve.

Facing mortality so young meant not only did I break away from any new friends I'd begun making, who couldn't really understand what was going on in my head, but I also felt distance from myself too. I came to see my life as being split into two distinct parts: Before Cancer and After

Death. The person I was – happy and carefree – had gone, barely recognisable now, replaced with a determinedly serious woman. I became keenly aware that everything has an end point; now, I am always battling a ticking clock.

Travelling made me feel alive, far too busy to acknowledge any grief I was feeling, and I think I believed that if I kept moving physically then time couldn't keep up with me. It was escape in the very literal sense, but it also gave me a definite purpose at a time when I felt that life really had none at all.

The whole process was all about the external world. I would tick off places from the contents of the books I'd read with my mum, as though they were joint ambitions we had to complete together. To support myself, I took jobs anywhere I could – working in fairgrounds with ex-convicts and drifters, slaving away in call centres with other foreign acquaintances also prepared to work for well below the minimum wage. I took every overtime shift going, saved every penny I could, then blew it all by taking myself off to another place and starting afresh there.

The people I met on my journeys wouldn't ever know me as the girl who lost her mum; instead, I would be a head-down serious worker, devoted to my job to the exclusion of everything else. I chose not to make friends, never wanting to establish bonds that could be broken. It wasn't a healthy lifestyle, but it worked.

Until I came back to my dad's.

I was there to stay for a few weeks while I sorted my next visa, but Dad quickly pulled the world from under my feet once more. I was told I had to remove the last of all of my belongings from his house – none could remain, even in the attic. I was advised that if they did they would be destroyed. I felt like a teen again, being forced to choose between seeing my boyfriend and staying at home. It paralysed me.

And so my travels came to a grinding halt. I found a storage locker to rent and took a job on a local newspaper, intending to stay just long enough to pay for a couple of years' worth of self-storage fees. I moved in with my then boyfriend and his mum, sharing his single bed. The contents of my whole life now sat gathering dust in a storage room that measured 2.5 square metres.

Working at the paper, I soon got sucked into a world of telling other people's stories. I was quickly promoted for my work ethic and knack for getting to the root of even the most difficult stories. One of my first jobs was to do what's known as a 'death-knock', turning up, unannounced, on the doorstep of a family whose young son had just died of cancer, to get a comment from the father. I did it without complaint and even got invited to the funeral. Perhaps he could sense my own loss when I asked him for heartfelt words, knowing none would ever suffice.

Other than the man whose family I lived with – a rekindled romance from what seemed like a lifetime ago – I had no friends to see on my days off. The itinerant lifestyle of the last few years, coupled with the possessive nature of my former relationship, as well as moving to England for university, had not allowed me to maintain any meaningful friendships. But I did have professional contacts who would call and tell me secrets about their colleagues 'off-the-record', giving me regular scoops. I wasn't happy, but with my meagre salary I soon rented a small flat with my boyfriend in Prestatyn where I could fall asleep listening to the gulls cawing at my windowsill.

I turn my back on the sea, determined to get more miles walked. I have no plan about where I am going to sleep at the end of the day or, in fact, for the entire journey. I also realise, with a growing annoyance, that this entire time my pilgrim passport has stayed firmly in my backpack, and despite the distance I've covered it still only contains a single stamp from the start point.

The light is starting to fade and I feel a cool chill on my neck that makes me shiver. I try to focus on the trail ahead, but disturbing thoughts begin to press their way into my mind, relentlessly. Walking on, I come to a fork in the mud-splattered path and suddenly get a waft of the scent of old leaves decaying. I feel immediately agitated.

Suddenly I find myself back in Wales during an autumn many years ago. I'd been out to celebrate a colleague's birthday and had such a great time that I came back to the flat I shared with my then boyfriend a little later than planned. He accused me of cheating. He grabbed my wrists so tightly I could feel them bruising. He smacked me on the cheek and berated me for being a whore. I was so scared I ran out into the rain without even putting on a pair of shoes, my feet scratching on piles of fallen, damp leaves. I nearly got away that time. I ran into a couple who stopped to ask if I was okay and if they could help me. I paused. It was the only time in my desperate situation that the truth – or part of it – had ever been exposed to anyone. I was almost tempted to accept, but then he came up behind me and placed a hand so tenderly on my shoulder you'd never have suspected the scene I'd just run from. To them it must have looked as though he was coming to see me back to safety, to take me under his warm, strong arm for my own protection, and I willed myself to believe the lie. But the grip I felt around me was a secret threat for what would happen to me, and – more importantly – to them, should I try and raise an alarm.

And so I found myself led away, resigned to my role in any relationship going forward. Accepting whatever my lot was as though it was penance for something I'd unknowingly done. By that point, abandonment was already cemented in my psyche as something always threatened and to be avoided at all costs; desertion was what I deserved; and asking and taking help was perhaps the most dangerous thing I could do.

The sun is beginning to drop lower in the sky now, casting a salmon-coloured fringe around the edge of the treeline, like a chromatic aberration in a photograph. As I walk, a raven calls its eerie croak, and my footsteps are accompanied with a sucking reverb as the ground becomes boggy.

Since I first discovered wild camping – the ability to lie down and sleep wherever you choose – I've never been concerned about walking well into nightfall and finding a bed in a ditch. Over the years it has not only been something of a hobby I could write about, but also an act that offered salvation from any of life's challenges. Sleeping wild would, in the past, temporarily turn the off-switch on some of my most negative thoughts.

Yet since I ended my latest relationship, quit my job, and walked out on life as I knew it, I inexplicably find myself less keen on being alone in the darkness. Instead of peace, it now provides uninterrupted silence for my inner critic to scream at me. As the last of the sun crescents over the horizon ahead, a flock of black-backed gulls swarm into the air, almost taunting me with their vast numbers as I march on, alone.

I find myself on a permissive path, moving through a woodland of Norwegian spruce, most of which appears to glow ethereally in the orange dusk. A few have been overrun with ivy that seems to be holding them in an embrace, though I note some have had their crowns smothered by it and now risk toppling over in turbulent weather. I look at the map and resolutely declare to no one that I will make it to Tremeirchion. But as I emerge from the small spindly copse, I enter a farmer's field where maize crops tower above me and any path leading the way forward has been obliterated.

I plough headfirst into the maze, getting slapped in the face by huge, thick leaves larger than my own hand. Whisps of yellow corn silk stick to my sweaty face as I become increasingly exasperated by the barrier in front of me. I feel my legs and arms getting scratched and grazed, I want to turn back many times, but something keeps pushing me onwards. I stop to check my location on the GPS on my phone and find I am only halfway through the field. Exhausted, I begin stamping the stalks at their bases, taking out on them an anger I didn't even know I was capable of. I swear and shout. With each vocalisation I feel a slight relief, until I finally reach the fence line and a stile that will see me out.

If my earlier definition of a pilgrimage was right, that it had to be a walk defined by toughness and obstacles, then this is certainly the first physical proof that this path is legitimate. The second hurdle comes quickly afterwards, as I cut through a kissing gate into a field stocked with cows.

Growing up with cattle as a mainstay of any walk, I've always maintained that cows are not in the least bit danger-ous. This herd, however, seems edgy, perhaps picking up on my own anxiety. I stride towards them with purpose, desperate to reduce the distance between me and my end goal. But, while some of them move, one stays put, her eyes fixed on me determinedly.

I start yelling, hoping my voice will convince her that I am human. She doesn't care, because a second later she runs, straight at me, and to my horror the others follow. Every piece of advice I've ever had about how to deal with cows tells me that I categorically should not run. It's a motto I've lived by my entire existence. Even when things get bad, impossibly bad, you should never run. But this time, I ignore it. I run so hard and so fast towards the fence that my chest feels as if it will explode. Barbed wire stands between me and the safety of an adjacent field, and I can feel the ground reverberating behind me as the cows gain pace, coming closer and closer. And then, though moments before I'd felt so tired I could barely lift another limb, I suddenly find the strength to vault over it.

I land with a thud into some stinging nettles and the cows jostle and try to push through the fence into the empty field where I now stand. They are raging, some even trying to push down a telegraph pole that stands on their side of the fence, while I watch in disbelief. It feels every bit as allegorical as Bunyan's *Pilgrim's Progress* – an actual beast guarding my hope for redemption.

I stumble along the field I am not supposed to be in, feeling slightly liberated and extremely shaken. A few minutes later I reach the road that leads to a flyover across the A55 at the top of Rhuallt Hill.

I am tired and lost. But I finally find the courage to ask someone for help.

I take out my phone and call my dad.

Back when Mum discovered she had a very low chance of surviving her cancer, but still looked and acted the same as she always had, she picked me up from the train station in Chester. By then I was at university and living in Preston, and Mum was taking me out for a meal. At first our conversation was filled with pleasantries. She tried to remain upbeat about her prognosis, and I tried not to show any upset, for her sake.

As we approached the turnoff for Caerwys, something in me decided to ask her what she would want us to do if she didn't make it. What should we do with her when she'd gone? Without much thinking she immediately said she wanted to be cremated; she didn't want a grave that could be left to fall into ruin. Instead, she said, she'd like her ashes to be scattered on a mountain in Snowdonia – Tryfan, perhaps the most striking of them all, 'so that when you or your brother come back here when you're older, if you've left, you'll drive down this road, as we always do, and on a clear day you'll see it and think of me'.

At the time I didn't realise that I was the only one to have had that conversation with her. She never thought to leave a will. But when she died and the funeral director asked the inevitable, I was the only one with any answer. So we went with that. I remember years later telling a boyfriend about it when we were driving into Wales to visit my dad, and he somehow thought that we'd literally scattered mum's ashes in a layby where a coffee and burger van was parked up.

But now, after my ordeal with the cows on the pilgrimage, when Dad comes to pick me up and takes me to his house not far away, I look to the side of the road and I think of her smiling face, somehow in on the joke.

Over the days that follow, I begin to feel a little renewed. Having Dad all to myself, without relationships in either of our lives getting in the way, we have focus. For me, that focus is on continuing my chosen pilgrim route.

He doesn't quite understand why I need to do it, but he does decide to support me in my quest to Bardsey Island.

We become a team. He drives me back to the A55 flyover and from there I walk as much as I can, until I need to call him again and he comes and picks me up.

Sometimes he joins me for a section, such as the journey through St Asaph, the cathedral city. It's named after the ecclesiastical thirteenth-century building, dedicated to St Asa, thought to be the smallest Anglican cathedral in Britain. Before it stood here there was a church built by St Kentigern, a saint from the sixth century (often called St Mungo in Scotland) who, it is said, stood in the nearby River Elwy up to his waist to pray. It is his name that was given to the hospice up the road where Mum and I held hands as she took her last breath.

Other times, Dad leaves me to walk by myself, with a sandwich and a 'just in case' meeting point (in case my phone battery runs out or my signal fails).

I continue onwards, with the silent assurance of my dad somehow being with me as I wander through huge swathes of countryside to Llansannan, once home to Gwilym Hiraethog, the Welsh bard and poet. I take in the tree-hewn sculptures of pilgrims on the section that leads through

Cleiriach and the woods at Pandy Tudur, their wooden bodies morphing out the sides of old fir tree stumps to point me in the right direction.

Bound for Rowen, I pass Eglwysbach, which translates as 'little church'. It's a village that sits above the Afon Conway waterway. As we pass it in the car on the way to my next day's starting point, Dad and I recall the time Mum made us all drive out here so she could pick up a new herbal remedy she had read about, made by a woman who lived in the forest. Neither of us remembers exactly what it was supposed to do.

After I, alone, complete the day section that cleaves through Penmaenmawr, where the Druids' Circle – a crop of spiritual stones from 3000 BC – serves to remind me of the beliefs that existed long before Christianity, I ask Dad on pick-up if he can take me to see my brother, who lives nearby.

After Dad drops me off, my brother and I end up spending hours reminiscing about Mum – the good and the bad. He tells me that Dad once said that 'the wrong parent had died' and I feel a stabbing pain in my chest at the thought that he felt less loved by us both.

At Abergwyngregyn, where two trail options are offered, I opt to head inland to take in Snowdonia; to feel Mum's gaze from the top of Tryfan. Though the trail doesn't pass her mountain, I cannot imagine choosing the path that would wilfully depart from the National Park that is her final resting place.

When Dad deposits me at Deiniolen he gets out of the car to enjoy a view of Snowdon that, in nearly a lifetime of living here, he says he has never seen. He wants to walk with me, but his feet aren't up to the job. We part ways, and I spend the entire span of daylight wandering through the past – both mine, and the region's.

I walk amid the slate mines that once supported a giant industry and which I visited on school trips when I was younger. I pass the well-known Pete's Eats café in Llanberis where we used to come every summer as a treat. The nearest my mum ever got to being a climber was sitting there having a giant mug of tea. I used to stare open-mouthed at some of the photographs of adventurers adorning the walls, though was told by her that it was something someone like me would never do. I would never be strong enough.

I crest the hills opposite the Nantlle Ridge, the site of my first ever solo wild camp, the walk that in a way made me into the adult I'd become. It had happened many years earlier when, working at an outdoor magazine, I pitched a feature in which I would go into the wild alone. I was told I couldn't, shouldn't and wouldn't be able to do this as a lone woman – 'it's too dangerous,' I was informed. When I pointed to an earlier article penned by a male writer about the same subject, there was a reassertion that I was defined by a different set of rules because of my gender – the same message I had received from my parents as a teen. It made me adamant I would go. And so I did. And though all manner of things went wrong – I got chased by sheep, eaten alive by midges, and ran out of water far from a water source – I did it. And from that day on my gender was not questioned there again. I didn't know it at the time, but it undoubtedly planted a seed of confidence in me that, over the years that proceeded it, slowly began to germinate.

After admiring the ridge, I climb Moel Tryfan, a tiny hill (just 427 metres in height). Named after the much taller one that's home to my mum's ashes, it is the place where Darwin first understood – as he walked amid 'boulders of foreign rock' – that this peak had once been at the bottom of the ocean. It's a destination ignored by most walkers, due to the extensive slate mining that takes place on its flanks. I walk by heaps of the iconic purple slabs of rock; they look so tough, with their sharp corners and spiked edges, but are really very brittle, and shatter easily when heavy pressure is placed on them from above. I empathise with their make-up. I see myself reflected everywhere in this landscape.

Reaching Penygroes is a pivotal moment: I realise I am now on the final coastal stretch to Bardsey. The end is just a few days away.

Dad supports me all the way down the Llŷn Peninsula, as I climb the triple-pronged summit of Yr Eifl (home to the best-preserved Iron Age hillfort in Europe called Tre'r Ceiri – which translates to Settlement of the Giants); race the tide when taking the beachside route to Trefor; and visit multiple churches. There is Capel Uchaf with its lavishly carved figures, bright interior painted wood and celestial scene on the ceiling. St Beuno's at Clynnog Fawr, named after one of the earliest Welsh saints, whose nearby well rivals St Winefride's as being the 'Lourdes of Wales', is home to an ancient box carved from ash that pilgrims following the same route as me would have left offerings in to pay for their sins. And St Mary's Church, now housing the Llŷn Maritime Museum – a small collection of paintings, artefacts and photographs dedicated to the coastal history of the area.

At Nefyn I tell Dad I need to finish the trail alone, without his help. He reluctantly leaves me to finish this pilgrimage how I started it. Solo.

When the day came to finally scatter my mum's ashes on Tryfan, a few weeks after her death, my brother and Dad were noticeably upset. For at least a couple of weeks, all that physically remained of her was sat in a dark green plastic container in the corner of the hallway. I was uncomfortable knowing it was there, locked up inside a house. She would have hated it.

So I pushed for a resolution, to allow her to be set free.

The last time she came to see me was up in Preston, just before she was due to start a round of chemotherapy and before I was set to head to Delaware. She took me to a shop where she spotted a long black dress that she made me try on. This wasn't a formal gown. Either side it had splits that went right up to my thighs, the fabric was a double-layered lace stitched to look like thousands of spider webs, with a purposely made tear across my chest, beneath the spaghetti straps.

When I came out of the changing room she told me she could see me wearing it standing barefoot on the side of a mountain. I laughed dismissively. And we left the store without a purchase.

But later that day she presented me with it. I would know when to wear it, she said.

At her funeral I had decided the time was right. She had demanded no one wear black, but I knew she would appreciate my flouting the rules to wear this dress. Even as I walked into the chapel, I could hear people murmur how inappropriate a choice of attire it was. When I stood up to read a poem some looked away in disapproval, but for once I let them be unhappy with my choice. It was not for them, it was for her.

115

The day we went to set her free on Tryfan we climbed up the slopes as high as we could, so that we could see the sea in the distance. Then my dad and brother each took a turn to release a part of her into the air. As the container was handed to me by my brother, he looked away, his face stained with tears.

But I didn't feel like crying. To me this wasn't like her funeral – the time when she was locked into a plywood box and sent on a journey into the cremation chamber to be transformed into dust. She was finally going to be released again.

As I tipped the last of her into the mountain air, to complete her liberation into nature, a gust of wind picked up and whipped some of the ashes into my face and hair. I heard my family gasp, but I didn't care; it felt like one final embrace. I called some words into the air and looked up to see a raven drift overhead before disappearing behind the mountain.

It was perfect.

Having fallen into a comfortable rhythm with my dad, it feels odd to be on the trail knowing that in the evening I will still be alone. I hire a small caravan for a couple of nights to have somewhere warm to end my journey and wait for the ferry over to Ynys Enlli, Bardsey Island.

The last two days of the hike feel like an ever-growing crescendo leading up to the moment when I will finally reach the patch of land known as the island of 20,000 saints. Such was the fame of the isle as a sacred and ancient place of power in years gone by that during the pontificate of Pope Callixtus II, between 1119 and 1124, he decreed that three walks to Bardsey was the equivalent of walking to Rome; doing so would give the pilgrim a virtual guarantee of sainthood. So much was this belief held true that often people walked there to die, assuming that by being buried there they automatically attained access into heaven (hence the popularity – 20,000 graves for 20,000 souls).

Crossing over the sea to reach it is never guaranteed, even when booking in advance with the one man who takes people on the twenty-minute ride on his small boat. A farmer, gruff and direct, he is out a lot and so a recorded message plays when you call him, with updates on the sailings advising whether or not they are possible over the next two days.

The Welsh name for Bardsey translates as 'Island of Currents' – clearly a safe crossing has never been a certainty – but the English name refers to it as isle of the Bards. As a singer, on a mission to re-find my voice, I convince myself that everything will make more sense when I get there.

I pass the Tŷ Coch Inn at Porthdinllaen in the early morning on my second-to-last day on the trail. Situated in

117

a tiny hamlet of houses right on the sand, it's a hostelry only reached by those prepared to walk to it. At that hour, it is closed and boarded up, to protect against the wind and tides – as opposed to would-be thieves. It was originally built as a vicarage in the 1800s until the Reverend John Parry Jones relocated to an alternative house built beside his church at Edern, further inland, and left the former to his housekeeper to run as an inn to serve boatbuilders in the bay. She did so, and despite it at one time competing with four others in the same location, this was the only pub to survive.

The end of my journey is becoming tantalisingly close. After Tudweiliog, I decide to skip the optional visit to the church at Llangwynnadl so that I can enjoy the coast for as long as possible. Growing up by the sea as I did, but no longer being close to it, I find I yearn for the waves and wind whenever I get the chance. I live close to a river now, which satiates some longing for water, but nothing beats the deafening roar and unbridled power of the sea playing out for all my senses.

Rain begins to fall when I reach Porthor, where surfers float above the froth of endlessly breaking waves. I envy them their pews. I know I could make quicker progress if I remain high, but the beach is known as Whistling Sands due to the molecular make-up of the grains, causing them to squeak beneath the weight of each footstep. I want to hear it. And so I make my way to the shore and take off my boots. My voice may not yet allow a tune, but here on a beach from my past, my feet can at least provide it.

Finally I head inland, crossing farm fields and following a winding stream to the fishing village at the Welsh Land's End, Aberdaron, somewhere my mum and dad would take us to on holiday as children. Here in the church of St Hywyn I take a minute to pause by a pile of stones, similar to the cairns seen on the Camino de Santiago. They are carried by pilgrims on their hike as a symbol of a burden, like Christian's in *The Pilgrim's Progress*, and are left behind when deliverance occurs at the end of their journey.

I have no such symbolic object myself, even my pilgrim passport remains unstamped, and so I wander around the impossibly steep graveyard, gazing out to Bardsey Island, where I truly believe my moment, my chance of clarity and my journey's end, will come.

Y Gegin Fawr, the Great Kitchen, is a fourteenth-century white-walled building where pilgrims could rest and claim a meal and a drink before they undertook what was then a perilous journey to the island. Now it still serves as a café, though when I go in for food they tell me I am too early to get anything. While I wait, I call to check on my boat crossing.

The news is bad.

A weather front has changed everything and, not mincing his words, the farmer says it would be life-threatening to go out there. I retire to my caravan and wait.

After three days of sitting in hope, I know I have to leave. Rather than improving, the weather is getting worse. Even though the showers occasionally subside and the sky becomes awash with rainbows, the wind is far too strong, and the waves too high and rough, and the prediction is that this will last for weeks.

I have work waiting for me, and bills to pay, and so I decide that the next day I will head home. Returning, as I had arrived here in Wales, a failure.

On my last morning I go for a final walk, telling no one, on a mission to follow the land as far as it extends before it relents to the sea.

I take the coastal path up to Mynydd Mawr, where a former Victorian coastguard lookout hut now houses volunteers in the summertime to teach visitors about the local bird life. Below it, a faint trail leads down to the remains of radar platforms used in the two world wars by the RAF and, beneath them, the depressions from Bronze Age hut circles complete the palimpsestic landscape.

I walk first down to Braich y Pwll and stand above Bardsey Sound, gazing at the island that, for me, isn't meant to be. Sheep eye me with a perturbed chewing of cud, while opportunistic orange-beaked choughs probe the soil for the earthworms that I may have disturbed with my footsteps.

It is only when I check the map to find the best route back to town that I notice the gothic print denoting a site of archaeological or historic significance. At the cleft of some cliffs to the south of where I am standing, on the southern slope of Trwyn Maen Melyn, the map shows St Mary's Well, known locally as Ffynnon Fair. It is a natural spring that folklore says sits below the tide line, yet always remains free of brackish water. The reality is that it is too high to ever be engulfed by the waves – its location, cleaved like a triangle into the cliffside, makes it unreachable even at high tide – but it can easily be mistaken for a rockpool.

It is said to be one of the holiest of all Welsh sites, and its draw probably predates the Christian pilgrimages. Its popularity has never diminished. In 1904, newspapers tell of a sixteen-year-old girl who perished in pursuit of her sadly ill-timed venture to find it.

Despite the documented danger, I want to see the well with my own eyes, to taste the water inside it. Pilgrims would once wash in it to ensure their journey on rough water would be blessed. And while I know I won't be crossing the sound here, I also know that, for me, there are definitely still stormy seas ahead, and any chance of help navigating them seems worth the risk.

With the voice of my ex in my head demanding that I tell someone what I am doing before I head out on this 'madcap adventure', I make my way down the criss-cross of lichen-topped stone paths, the grass worn thin by those who have gone before me.

Shuffling down on my bottom, I near a runnel where the tide is racing in and crashing against the water-blackened rocks. In a leap of faith I jump over the waves and grip a rocky flake in both hands. I climb upwards, unsure of where exactly I am headed. I allow the foot and handholds to guide me. When I stop to get my breath I see slithers of green on some rocks around 10 metres away – a sure sign of freshwater.

In that moment, nothing else matters at all: not my ex; not the cancelled ferry to Bardsey and my failed pilgrimage; not even my mum's death, her funeral and the aftermath; not my complex relationship with my father. I am thinking only about the rock under my fingertips. Its roughness sanding away my coarse edges, the scorch of the wind echoing in my ears and silencing any guilt or doubt. I feel the strength in my arms as adrenaline courses through my body. Then I am there.

I arrive at the watery shelf, lined with exquisitely vivid viridian weed, and drink the water from my cupped hands.

I look over to the island that I wasn't meant to reach while shearwaters dance in the air, forming monochrome crosses in my vision. It isn't the end to the North Wales Pilgrim's Way I had anticipated. There are no ruins of monostatic houses, or Grade II listed buildings; no chaplain to talk to.

I have spent two weeks on the trail and collected no stamps. Instead, I have recollected some vital memories. A huge wave rolls in below where I am standing and its spray launches upwards and splashes on my cheek. Stood here, above the crashing ocean, a holy island in front of me, and the stories of my past behind, contemplating my return to the safety of solid ground I feel, for the first time in decades, a little more like myself.

FOUR

Renewal

When I was ten my parents both worked full-time, so for most school holidays I stayed with my dad's mum – the only grandparent we had. Granny had dutifully moved closer to help my parents with childcare. Like me, she used to love writing, though never professionally. She was the first pensioner in her cul-de-sac to invest in an electronic typewriter that came with a screen – an early example of a word processor. She would sometimes let me use it when I became bored of watching the same cycle of videos she had on offer – *Blackadder, Yes Minister* and the 1968 musical *Oliver!* I would use it to write made-up stories and delight in watching my words spool out from a small blue screen onto a clean piece of white paper, the actual manifestation of an idea I'd had, magically transformed into a physical item that I could hold in my hand.

On a particular day in July, while Granny was talking to her neighbours outside, I let myself into the small boxroom where her typewriter was kept, intent on writing a piece about witches. On the desk beside it, I spotted a pile of printed papers. I picked them up and began to read.

They documented a story about a girl who married her childhood sweetheart in a whirlwind ceremony before he was sent off to fight in a war. We'd started to learn about the Second World War in school, so to me it was a familiar subject.

I was swept up in the tale of this couple whose fiery relationship, and marriage, played out against the back-drop of the world ending. The man left to do his duty in France, sending back regular letters to his beloved. Then, suddenly, the letters stopped.

A few days later the girl received a telegram reporting that her husband was missing in action, presumed dead, when his plane was shot down, falling into the icy waters of the Channel below.

The story didn't end there. Instead it joined the widow many years later – now remarried with two children, and even grandchildren, of her own. One day she unearthed a diary recording that the night before his death her deceased pilot husband had been out with some French girls, one of whom was described with particularly lascivious detail.

Instead of being distraught at his apparent betrayal – she felt an inexplicable sense of happiness that this young man had enjoyed, in his words, 'one of the best nights of my life'. She explained how it was somehow a source of solace to know he had lived a little before his life was cut short. I didn't understand how she could forgive him for his cheating. But then, I was just a child.

Only at the end of the story did I realise that the girl in it was my granny. It was the first time I had seen her as a woman, rather than just a grandparent. It exposed me to the fact that adults have had their own lives before we ever existed, and it shocked me. I never looked at her the same way again.

Later, my mum told me that Granny never truly accepted that her first husband had died. His body was never found, after all. She chose instead to believe that he had survived, washed ashore in France, suffering from amnesia. That he had lived a whole new life on the other side of the water.

The end of my pilgrimage in Wales left me pondering the healing power of water. I already knew about Lourdes, that sleepy town in the Pyrenees, which overnight became the number-one pilgrim destination in Europe when, in 1858, a fourteen-year-old called Bernadette Soubirous claimed to have seen the Virgin Mary at the Grotto of Massabielle.

The Welsh version in Holywell predated it by several hundred years, and before arriving there I had learned of the life-giving properties that holy water is claimed to possess. I'd read too of another water source in Marston, Buckinghamshire, discovered by John Schorne during a drought in the thirteenth century. It was said to be the site of miracles – even Henry VIII visited it twice on a pilgrimage before he banned the practice.

But that day on the cliffside ledge at St Mary's Well, I felt something stir when the cold water touched my skin. Wild – or open water – swimming is something that has been growing in popularity in Britain, at a similar rate as pilgrimages, for at least a decade. It's featured with such regularity in the newspapers' travel sections that there are even spoof articles circulating online that make fun of the clichéd narratives.

I had managed to avoid the craze until this point, too scarred by memories of enforced fun in the freezing sea waters at Colwyn Bay and Rhyl as a child to be tempted. But after changing my life so completely – ending my relationship, quitting my job and starting therapy – I decided I needed to push my comfort zone and embrace new things.

Among the many activities I undertook – qualifying as a Zumba instructor and teaching a single lesson, trying roller skiing and spending the night on a portaledge suspended from the roof of a building – just a couple of months after returning from my Welsh pilgrimage I decided to try open water swimming.

I chose the River Thames in rural Berkshire, close to where I lived, to overcome my fear. I waited until the weather had settled into a warm cycle, so that – I hoped – it would be slightly less bracing.

On the day in question I went for a long walk first to work up a sweat and make the cold seem more appealing.

When I finally stepped in, wearing only my underwear, it was so cold I thought I might stop breathing. I wandered in up to my knees, then hesitated. After several seconds I pushed myself further in, and winced as I felt the icy chill grip my hips. I was determined not to be beaten. When it reached my shoulders I truly believed I could go no further. But then a common tern plunged into the river beside me, emerging seconds later in a theatrical flutter of feathers and water droplets with a fish in its mouth.

I found an inner resolve, took a deep breath and submerged myself completely. The last thing to be taken was my hair, at first spooling above my body like eel grass floating in the current, until finally it too disappeared beneath the water.

When I resurfaced I felt renewed. The rest of the day I carried that feeling with me, hungry for more.

I had a feeling that I was about to begin another adventure. I was right. The invitation came as a text message from a man I'd met a couple of years earlier who would soon become a regular feature on the next part of my journey.

When we first met I barely gave The Scientist a second glance. Everyone told me he was a 'good guy': intelligent, kind and giving too. It didn't matter. I was in a relationship, and deeply ensconced in my own personal turmoil, trapped in the four walls of my existence. He was older than I was.

On our second meeting in a busy event in London a couple of months before I went to Wales, something changed. I was free and single. There had been an undeniable energy that seemed to electrify our conversation. Other people who were in the room seemed to notice it too and, despite us trying to keep our words to ourselves, they seemed drawn to us and attempted to join in. It was as though they were eager to plug in to this invisible surging current.

When we parted ways that night, we both held each other's glance for just that bit too long. This had been more than just another conversation. We kept in touch over email for a few weeks afterwards. The content was playful, and at the time seemed like harmless flattery.

Much like me, The Scientist was not often in one place for very long. His work called for him to travel across the world, on expeditions to places even I had never heard of, spending weeks at a time on the high seas or in vast tracts of forest collecting data.

We had exchanged numbers over email in case we could meet up when we were both in the same country, but it had never materialised into anything. That was until quite unexpectedly he asked me if I could meet him for a drink in London.

It was only to be one drink, starting in the late afternoon. No mention of food, no talk of a late finish. Before we met up – even on the day – flirtatious exchanges occurred, each beep of my phone making my stomach flutter as though filled with a kaleidoscope of marsh fritillaries. I thought it was the sensation of anticipation – my adrenaline sending increased blood to my muscles and away from my tummy in excitement. I would later learn this is also a symptom of social anxiety disorder.

We had both, unplanned, turned up with a gift for one another. He gave me a copy of Ernest Hemingway's *A Moveable Feast*, I handed over a copy of my book, *Wild Nights*.

We laughed a lot, moved quickly from drinking tea to ordering a bottle of wine, and then stumbled across London on a mission to find dinner.

As the night went on I found myself hanging on to his arm – both to steady myself in my growing state of intoxication, and to allow myself to feel another human being against my skin.

When we sat in a small late-night café eating toast and avocado, while the staff kept reminding us they needed to close, he made me blush repeatedly.

I excused myself to go to the bathroom and looked at my reflection in the mirror. My make-up was already a little smudged, my cheeks and chest were pink from the wine, and my eyes were unable to focus properly. I looked at the clock. We'd been talking for more than five hours.

When I returned he was looking at his phone, a concerned look on his face, but he quickly put it away when I sat down. 'You're a bit much,' he said as he gestured to the waiter that he would pay the bill and hurriedly led me out towards the Underground Station. I wasn't sure whether to take it as a compliment or an insult, but the lights of the city were beginning to spin.

We were both going in different directions to our respective homes. He said goodnight and waved as he ran through the barriers to catch his train headed north. He looked back at me and stopped and smiled. On impulse I squeezed through the turnstile without a ticket so that I could give him a hug. I left in a fit of drunken giggles, my body made warm from our embrace.

On the way home he kept texting me messages packed full of innuendo and *double entendre*. As the wine began to wear off and I headed further west, back to my lonely house, I bathed in the endless stream of wordplay, unable to stop the game.

Buoyed by the beginning of something new on the horizon, and refreshed from my time on the North Wales Pilgrim's Way, I plotted my next walk with glee rather than a sense of obligation. Unlike my other wanderings this far, I wanted the next route to avoid overt connotations of death or flight. I wanted to undertake a pathway that promised growth and – I dared to hope – joy.

After ending my last walk by water, I opted to continue on this course, and choose one in the far north of Britain, in Scotland, that would take in not one but two islands surrounded by tides. Called the St Columba's Way, it's 420 kilometres long and runs between the ancient pilgrimage town of St Andrews, on the Fife coast on the eastern edge of Scotland, and the island of Iona in the Inner Hebrides to the west of the mainland.

Once the site of a vast and imposing cathedral, St Andrews was so named as it is said to be home to the remains of the fisherman disciple of Jesus who is the patron saint of Scotland and whose cross, or saltire, is emblazoned on the flag of the country in contrasting blue and white. For 400 years this small town was one of the most important Scottish pilgrim destinations in Scotland, and indeed Europe, being one of only two places on the continent where the remains of an apostle were believed to be laid to rest at the time. That was until 1559, slightly later than in England (and through it Wales), when the notoriously violent Scottish Reformation happened, leaving the cathedral ruined, three men burned as martyrs, the status of ecclesiastical capital removed, and the town left in a dilapidated state. Nowadays, its devotees are golfers who come to hit balls against the backdrop of the decaying towers of the once grand religious structure.

A month's worth of walking was more than I could spare financially; I had assignments booked in that I needed to take. So I decided to walk a truncated version of the path, focusing on the western reaches of the trail, which also traces two other routes: that of St Conan (one of St Columbus's followers) and the Stevenson Way, named after Robert Louis Stevenson, who famously penned the book *Kidnapped* – about a boy who is stolen by his uncle and put on a ship bound for the Carolinas of the USA, only to become shipwrecked on the Isle of Mull and make his way back home to Edinburgh. I choose to begin with a ferry ride from the mainland, then make my way across Mull, before taking another boat to Iona. I would explore by day and camp by night. I would be surrounded by water, itself governed by the moon, pushed and pulled in an endless and powerful cycle.

After Granny lost her first husband, she started to take more risks. She joined the army, rose through the ranks and took a posting to Cairo, a place where she would meet the man who would later become my grandad. Years after, when he died too – this time of cancer – she was now in her sixties and went even further down the adventure road. She bought a round-the-world ticket and travelled as far and wide as she could afford, trying bungee jumping, kayaking and riding on roller-coasters – all the things she was never allowed to do when she was married.

I learned from my dad that at one point when he and my mum first married, she'd lived in South America and nearly didn't come back. But my grandad didn't want to stay, hadn't liked the 'foreign food' and humidity, and by the time I knew her she was the picture of a dutiful housewife who did as she was told, never made a fuss, and never sought to show another side of herself other than the small, curly-haired, partially blind woman that the world took her to be.

I felt like I had started to become like my granny. I wanted more risk in my life. Inspired by a potential relationship with a man who made his living on the high seas, I decided to confront one of my biggest fears and learn how to dive.

The first time I tried it had been over a decade before, in Australia, on assignment for a backpacker magazine, when I'd taken a journey out to the Great Barrier Reef. The expedition leader insisted I do a 'try-dive' – basically, put on all the gear without the faintest idea of what everything did, climb under a boat, with weights pulling me down into the bottomless depths, and take the regulator out of my mouth just to show I could do so, before putting it back in. As soon as I stepped off the vessel I knew that in every way I was out of my depth. I looked into the sea and saw nothing but a huge blank of deep blue space that seemed to stretch forever beneath my flippered feet. One of the deckhands, seeing my reluctance, tried to push my head under and keep me there, forcing me to learn to breathe using a contraption I knew nothing about. I panicked, started choking and fought my way to the surface, deciding then that what lay beneath the waves was not mine for exploring.

Now, the prospect of panicking underwater didn't seem nearly so scary. I had lost – through my own actions – my job, my partner and my sense of self in the year before. So this would just be an extension of the constant feeling that things were out of control.

Yet on my first dive after signing up to a PADI course, I didn't feel helpless at all – quite the opposite. It was I alone who made the choice to leap into the water, ultimately responsible for my own survival. I understood the kit on my back, knew that the weights that hung around my waist were there to help rather than hinder, understood that if at any time I wanted to get out I only had to make a sign with my thumb.

Under the water everything was silent. Much like when I climbed on the cliffs at Trwyn Maen Melyn, the only thing I thought about was my slow movement through the water, regulated and controlled by my own steady breathing.

I felt brave, bold and indomitable.

But the thing about water is its propensity to distort reality. There are a number of times diving when I've forgotten this. I've looked off the back of a vessel and seen huge boulders capped with clusters of spiky sea urchins, convincing myself they were less than a metre away, working myself up by imagining I would impale myself on their amethyst needles, only to finally go under and realise they are much, much further away.

For a while, diving made me think that when I left the water I still had the effortless ability to control my life on land. Overcoming obstacles was as simple as breathing in and out. I was about to realise that this wasn't the case.

I take the sleeper train up to Crianlarich from London, and as I am rocked from side to side by the regular swaying of the carriages, messages fly between me and my Scientist with increasingly obvious intent. It is a change from my usual routine on this journey. Usually I'd have boarded, tired from a day of working solidly, and get straight into bed eager to shut out the rest of the world. This time I opt to sit in the restaurant car, surrounded by people excited to be headed home, or going on holiday. I sip white wine, as we had done on our first evening out together. He tells me he is in Norway and can see the Northern Lights outside his cabin, ebbing and swirling in emerald streams. I look out of my window and tell him I can see the same moon he can. He sends back multiple kisses.

Then come the acronyms: his way of saying what he'd like to do to me without stating it in words, in case – he claims – he has misread the situation. I feel as though I am being wooed like a heroine in a 1950s black-and-white movie.

His favourite is BKAO: Big Kisses All Over. It has been so long since I experienced anything close to that kind of affection, I lap it up. And then the photos begin. First, he sends pictures out of his window. Then of his bed. Next his own shadow, the outline of his body clear. Then, a picture of his erect penis.

I stop drinking my wine. I had enjoyed the flirtation and romance, had adored the talk of kisses, but now there was the hard reality of a sexual act, unexpectedly filling my screen. He asks me to send him a nude too.

I put my phone away. Uncertain of how I feel. And then the dutiful part of my brain kicks in and I worry that if I send no reply I will hurt his feelings. He'd taken a risk, and it was only fair to acknowledge that. So I just thank him and go to sleep feeling a little confused.

In the morning, when my train arrives at the small village in Stirling and the bus comes moments later to take me to the ferry dock, I feel sick from the alcohol I've enjoyed the night before. It is accompanied by a strange sense of guilt and uneasiness, as though I've woken up next to a stranger. My phone signal fades from four bars down to one, so I put it away in my pocket and throw myself into this pilgrimage.

There are many differing theories about St Columba, about the kind of person he was, the actions he took, and how he came to spread the word of Christianity in Scotland. One thing that everyone agrees on, though, is that he was from Ireland, one of the 'Twelve Irish Apostles' (a cohort of sixth-century saints who studied under a man called St Finnian, one of the fathers of early Celtic Christianity), and that he was then either banished, exiled or decided to take a pilgrimage to Scotland as a missionary.

I have read so many differing accounts that it is impossible to decide whether he was wholly good or wholly bad. But taking him at face value, he did seem a decent person. Travelling across the high seas in a currach made of wicker and animal skin, he was definitely keen as well as learned, and wanted to teach others too. He set up several churches around Scotland, returned to Ireland and did the same; wrote hymns, transcribed hundreds of books and, on Iona, his main base, which was known at the time as the Holy Isle, he turned his own monastery into a school for missionaries who could then go out and do 'good things' elsewhere in northern England.

He was strategic when making friends, ensuring he had relationships in key places so that even if people weren't converted to his way of thinking they would at least respect him and his work. He told stories of overcoming a 'water beast' in the River Ness in the year 565, in so doing saving the life of one of his followers (a miracle that to this day may be looked to as the origin of the myth of the Loch Ness Monster). His heroic status enabled him to befriend a pagan king, ensuring that his role in politics increased.

His route to (or from, depending on which way you are headed) Iona took the southern coast from Craignure dock, all the way around to Fionnphort over 65 kilometres of trail, with the path often invisible or badly formed. I have brought with me all the camping equipment to enable me to follow it, but when my ferry arrives the weather takes a turn.

A storm has blown in from the Atlantic, and weather warnings depicted as a smattering of yellow triangles for wind and rain appear plastered all over the forecast map.

Clouds sink down over the island's mountainous interior, shrouding them in a wispy cowl. At the same time, I receive an email offering me more work and, as it is so early in my freelance career, I feel I have to accept it. So I hire a bike and take the road instead, following the aforementioned St Conan's Way to halve the journey time.

I decide to split the route in two, with a wild camp in the middle, and set off encased head to toe in the pilgrim's uniform of the twenty-first century: Gore-Tex. At first, the terrain is simply a long strip of tarmac, lined with coniferous plantations and electric fences denoting private estates. The occasional silvery trunk of a birch tree breaks through the green and brown monoculture, while I am surprised by the unexplained dotting of purple from a rogue marsh orchid, the splashes of white created by dog-rose and pockets of wood sorrel. I stop for a break at Loch an Eilein where the now rugged peaks of Ben Buie and Beinn Mheadhoin form the more inspiring backdrop.

Cycling is still hard after my accident. I struggled to pedal to work in the months after it, and never allowed myself the free-falling sensation of whizzing down a hill without applying the brakes; I had become much more cautious. But something about the fresh air on Mull slowly overtakes my nerves with an unexpected exhilaration. I start to relax into my two-wheeled pilgrimage. I actually begin to smile.

As I pedal further, my phone signal returns and I feel my mobile quiver in my pocket. I stop to check it and see texts from The Scientist begging to be read.

During those five hours when we'd first properly got to know each other we discovered we had both lost our mothers. His loss had come more recently than mine, and I could see he was still reeling from the experience. Tears welled up in his eyes whenever she was mentioned. I had the knowledge to comfort him, felt it was my job to do so, and found myself uttering words I'd never allowed myself to say before: 'The pain doesn't ever go away, but you do get used to it.'

I liken the loss of my mum to having left an open wound in my chest. After some time, it begins to scab over, to get somehow repaired. I can start wearing clothing over the top of it and often forget that it's even there at all. Then, without warning, something will happen to tear off the layers in one quick motion and expose the gaping sore once more. And it stings.

Sometimes it's something very obvious, like the arrival of Mother's Day; at other times it can be as simple as a smell, like the scent of lilies that permeated the air of the hospice where Mum died. The smell was so strong, it still makes me nauseous.

I shared all of this with The Scientist, exposing more of me to him than I had to my own family. It had felt cathartic, but risky, though through his flattery and assurances I convinced myself I could trust him. Looking back now, the warning signs were all there for me to read even while I continued pedalling west, but his unwavering persistence overpowered my doubts, and his tender words of persuasion proved impossible for me to resist.

And so, the morning after my wild camp on the hillside above the shores of Loch Scridain, I lock myself in a tiny bathroom inside an inn. There I take and send what will be the first of many pictures and wait for a response.

I promise myself I won't look at my phone the entire time I pedal to the ferry at Fionnphort. I turn the alerts off to focus only on my surrounds. A small wreck of a wooden rowing boat catches my eye, its splintered remains abandoned on a boggy patch of ground, just off the side of the main thoroughfare. Cars begin to overtake me, bound for the same destination. The road starts to undulate, and I focus only on my movements, ensuring I hold my course firmly when speeding vehicles race alongside me. At the tiny crofting village of Bunessan, about nine kilometres from the port, I allow myself to steal a look at my phone, but there is no response. From feeling somehow in control, I suddenly feel used. Angry.

I throw my energy and exasperation into cycling, refusing to slow as I climb ascents, pushing my body to the point of pain, but then forbidding my hands to clasp the brakes on the steep descents. I am a fool.

I stop again at the granite church of St Ernan, named after Columba's uncle and former Prince of Donegal, just 1.6 kilometres from the ferry. The owner of the land here stipulated in the deeds when they were signed in 1897 that the church could only be opened for particular services, so it is locked, its bell core silhouetted against the clouds.

I chance another look at my phone. He has messaged back and I feel flushed with relief. He says he doesn't just like the picture, he LOVES it. There is a promise of another meeting ('we'd need three days, at least') and of a video call. He is going away on a voyage that will last eight weeks, so asks if I can make him a video that he can take with him, so that he is able to 'study' me in great detail.

It sounds as though he wants to capture me like I'm a specimen in one of his test tubes or the subject confined to the pages of his research papers. I feel a little empty, but then I have nothing else, no other potential relationships

144

on the horizon. I am never in a place long enough to form any attachments, and I am lonely. So I agree.

I arrive at Fionnphort exhausted from pushing myself so hard over the last few kilometres but still feel excited from my last interaction with The Scientist, and what I had promised to do for him.

I have often found my relationship with my body to be complex. In adult life it has too often been bound up with male aggression and used as a tool of control in relationships. There have been men who have told me to hide my shoulders, my legs, my back, along with parts of my personality. 'You were very flirty with him,' they might say, or 'You laughed too much.' One of my earlier boyfriends accused me of 'tempting' other men, meaning he would have to 'take care of it'. He once threatened to break a man's legs for getting along with me too well, and I knew first-hand what he was capable of. To distract him I let him take me to his house, where he forced me to have sex with him in such a manner that I whimpered in pain. After that I stopped talking to new people unless it was for a 'legitimate' reason. I began to cover up my legs and arms on the rare occasions when I ventured out. I began to hate physical intimacy with anyone after that experience, which angered later partners and caused roughness in more relationships. For several years I couldn't even bring myself to pretend to want it.

But now I am suddenly being told my body is beautiful. I am being encouraged to rediscover my sexual side in a way that gives me a sense of control. And I fall for it, hook, line and sinker.

When I arrive on Iona it is late afternoon and the shoals of day trippers that flood the island are heading home. In the story of St Columba and his eponymous trail, the end point comes here on the Sràid nam Marbh or 'Street of the Dead', which leads from the boat dock at Martyr's Bay to the old graveyard of Reilig Orain. Today, the end point for pilgrims is the thirteenth-century abbey that stands where Columba's church used to before it.

Back then, due to the numbers of pilgrims arriving, the place was specifically designed to lead people in a correct and measured manner to the church. Now a similar set of more officious arrows points the way to the cathedral, where one must pay to gain access.

Wild camping is essentially forbidden on this island, although the Land Reform Act of 2003 is supposed to give people the right to roam and sleep out under the stars across the whole of Scotland. I had tried to get into the single campsite before I came, but it was full. And any accommodation – of which there is a limited supply in such a tiny community (population: 120 year-round, a little more in the summer) – was long since booked up.

So I decide to wait until nightfall to pitch my tent, and plan to sneak a peek at the site of St Columba's teaching church by headtorch the following night. Until then I roam around on two wheels looking for clues from pilgrims past. I come to a ruined convent, which provided refuge for unmarried daughters, widows and illegitimate girls, a plaque explained. Nearby was a faint carving of a Sheela na gig (in Irish, Síle na gcíoch) or 'Sheila of the Breasts': a naked woman with her legs held apart and an oversized vulva – apparently a common symbol in Ireland that's said to ward off evil (though some theorists say it is to show the ugliness and sinful nature of a woman's lust). An oddly appropriate icon.

I wander amid smallholdings and find a field that has been left to grow wild between March and September to encourage secretive corncrakes to nest. These birds are red listed and migrate here from Africa. Their numbers have been hugely impacted by modern farming practices – specifically, combine harvesters that start on the edges of fields, scaring the birds into the middle where they and their nests are often located and then destroyed, unwittingly. It's hoped Iona will provide them with salvation too.

Finally, I head to the northern reaches of the island where a white-silted beach is named Traigh Ban nam

147

Manach, Gaelic for White Strand of the Monks. It's a site of one of the many massacres of monks by Vikings that took place over the thirty-year period between 795 and 825. The raids ravaged this place of worship, but never managed to wipe it out completely. The island did, and arguably still does, rely on the presence of religion to enable it to survive.

By moonlight I cycle to the south-west and the end of the road. There I leave my bike and continue on foot, heading south past Loch Staonaig, a rugged patch of water edged by toxic yellow irises and purple blooms of sea thrifts (often known as lady cushions). It's the only standing lake on the entire island. It's also the site of a mysterious death of a woman called Netta Fornario, a member of a supernatural cult who believed she could perform miracles using telepathy. Arriving here from London a few months before her demise, she was found dead, on 19 November 1929, at the age of thirty-three, lying on a mound of earth completely naked – save for a black cloak, a silver chain and a cross pendant that had apparently turned to black on her exposed skin. She was stretched out on top of a cross cut from grass with a knife (which itself lay next to her) and had unexplained scratches across her body. The cause of death was recorded as hypothermia, though many rumours flew across the island of a man in a black cloak and of strange azure lights dancing across the sky.

I lie down on the soft, waterlogged ground and look up at the clouded night. In my pocket my phone glows with a familiar blue light. The Scientist again. I'd told him I wished he was staying in the country a little while longer. 'It honestly makes me hate the idea of going away at all Xx,' he has replied.

Getting up, I move further along the Machair to the point known as St Columba's Bay or Port a'Churaich – Port of the Coracle – the place where the saint first landed on this island.

I set up my tent methodically on the last scraps of grass, oriented so that the wind that funnels in from the bay will hit the top of my pyramidal shelter and fly away into the interior of the island. I eat nothing, but instead gorge on the messages on my phone, satisfying another hunger that I had thought I could no longer feel.

I stir early to a clearer sky and crashing waves pummelling the pebble-strewn beach. I leave my hiding place and continue on my walk, seeking out the old marble quarry – the place from where it's believed the altar of the island's abbey came, streaked with yellow-green serpentine. Here, many years later, a landowner tried to make more money from the island's natural resources before abandoning them for being too expensive to remove.

St Martin's Caves are my next spot: a series of passage-ways hidden into the cliffs, which are only accessible at the lowest of tides. I cannot gain access that day, the water forbids it, so I continue on, unable to explore their rocky walls and remaining unclear as to who 'St Martin' actually was. Nearby is Spouting Cave, a naturally formed cleft in the cliffs that when the wind forces in waves from the west, directs water upwards in a plume like the blow of a whale. For me it does not perform.

By close of day I find a place known as Hermit's Cave, a circle of stones that is said to have formed the foundation of a cell – providing a retreat for monks or perhaps for Columba himself when silence was sought to pray. I linger here, listening to the wind and the waves.

By early evening, when it's dark enough, I sneak over the wall into the site of the nearby abbey to try to find the remains of Tòrr an Aba (Hill of the Abbot), once the location of Columba's writing hut. I hope it will bring me luck as a fellow scribe.

There are multiple written versions of Columba's character, and the longer I stay the more I discover. I learn that in Irish his name means dove, symbolic of peace and love; that he cut a striking figure and had a 'loud and melodious voice which could be heard from one hilltop to another'. I am drawn to the description of his tuneful voice and understand why such a man has become so revered.

But then I also hear other, more troublesome accounts. One speaks of how he banned women and cows from the island, stating that 'where there is a cow there is a woman, and where there is a woman there is mischief', so all the builders of his abbey were forced to banish their wives and daughters to a nearby isle known now as Eilean nam Ban (Woman's Island). Even worse, certainly for the protagonist, is a tale that states that in order to secure the foundations of his clay-and-wood church he believed he needed to bury one of his followers amid the walls to ensure its strength. One loyal acolyte was said to have volunteered immediately, to assure his place in heaven for such a sacrifice. But three days later they removed some stones and found him still alive. He recounted the existence of the promised place of true happiness, declaring hell not so bad, and demanded to be released. Upon which, so it's told, Columba demanded earth be thrown back into his eyes and mouth to stop him blaspheming further. Historians cannot find any conclusive evidence that this happened, though there is a hewn sculpture of a man's face frozen in horror, carved into the west crossing-arch in the choir at Iona Abbey.

It is confusing to find such diametrically opposed stories concerning the same person. It seems that everyone, no matter how saintly they appear, can be duplicitous.

On this small island I note that I am no longer acting like my usual serious self; I am giddy and blithe, lost to a feeling of righteousness, believing myself in the early stages of a new future with a kindred spirit. My body is no longer a thing to be feared or ashamed of, but formidable like the strong woman Sheila whose figure adorns the convent. I am renewed by this watery adventure, as I was back in the Thames months before.

On my last night on the island, I take myself down to the sandy shore and strip off all my clothes. Naked and unabashed I swim and call out into the waves. I roar up at the moon and bellow towards the tides, goading them to bring me their next test.

FIVE

Hermit

Saint Valentine was a man known and celebrated for his 'courtly love'. Thought to be a third-century Roman clergyman – either a priest or a bishop – one story has it that he would secretly perform Christian weddings, which would allow young men of military age to escape conscription. Sentenced to death for converting people, he was executed and martyred despite miraculously restoring the sight of the judge's young daughter. His skull, adorned with flowers, is exhibited in the Basilica of Santa Maria in Cosmedin, Rome. Other relics can be found in Whitefriar Street Carmelite Church, Dublin, which has itself become a popular destination for pilgrims. Because of Valentine, every year on 14 February in the Western world (the day, macabrely enough, on which he was executed) we are encouraged by the world's card shops, chocolate manufacturers and florists to show our feelings through giving gifts to those we wish to woo. But in Wales we have our own version of Valentine's Day, roughly two weeks earlier.

The story of Dwynwen, the fifth-century Welsh patron saint of lovers, is far less valiant and far more emotional, as I'd come to expect when reading about holy women. When she was young, she fell in love with a local boy called Maelon. But her father, King Brychan Brycheiniog, had already betrothed her to someone else, without her knowledge. Heartbroken, she fled to the solace of nature, deep in a forest, and there wept uncontrollably. An angel heard her cries and offered her a potion to ease her troubled heart. She took it, wanting to end her suffering, only to find that saving herself had frozen her beloved into a block of ice. God, like a genie, told her he would grant her three wishes. She first saved Maelon's life, then declared that all other lovers must be happier and luckier in romance than she had been, and, finally, she asked that she never be married. Her trio of wishes were granted and she lived out her days, alone, on a tiny tidal island off Anglesey called Llanddwyn (or, in English, The Church of Dwynwen).

Even now, amid the mudflats and dune grassland, the crumbling stone remains of her small convent can be seen on this craggy islet, along with a wishing well, a spring whose resident eels are said to predict the likelihood of a happy union if a couple dares to peer inside, and a bare memorial stone cross etched with her name, which translates to 'she who leads a blessed life'.

Much like Dwynwen, I never felt my purpose was to find love. When I was about eight, while my friends would feed their dolls bottles, I remember giving mine angular haircuts and fashioning their pretty dresses into more practical trousers. I would pretend to load them into the back of my car to drive them away from a bad relationship (I still don't know where that scenario had come from). Later, when others began to seek boyfriends and first kisses, I advertised in music shops hoping to join a band. They would talk about make-up and Wonderbras; I wore bondage trousers and dyed my hair green. A good night was singing at the top of my lungs to a song I loved, or spinning around a dancefloor as though I was twelve – I would never go out with romance in mind. Every relationship I had seemed to just happen upon me.

To this day most of my closest friends are men. I don't know why. Maybe it's because I grew up with an older brother and his friends were there so often that I never saw boys as an 'us and them' binary. Perhaps it's because I didn't enjoy the kind of things I was expected to do with girls – shopping, applying make-up, getting excited about cupcakes – and the activities I love to do (hiking, camping, kayaking) are seen as much less feminine and attract more men than women. Or maybe it's because I've always been more of a straight talker, I say things as I see them, and most of the other women I know don't seem to like that quality in another woman. In any case, I've always found relationships with women more tricky, more multi-layered.

From a very young age I also knew that marriage was not for me. My mum and dad met and married quickly when they were just twenty, though they waited for over a decade to start a family. And, although they stayed together until Mum died, there were rocky moments. Between their twenty-fifth wedding anniversary and Mum getting sick I remember distinctly one row in particular.

I must have been around fifteen and was sat in the living room when I heard terse words being exchanged. My mum was on the computer and my dad had seen an email she had sent to a man, a close colleague, that he felt had crossed some kind of line. As soon as I walked into the room they both fell silent, and I knew that something wasn't right.

In the days and weeks that followed I got piecemeal snippets of what had happened. My mum had been working on a new project, one that seemed to be making waves and a real difference in her industry, and that was starting to get executives to sit up and take notice. She had found an ally in this colleague, and someone who truly shared her passion for the subject. They worked together well, trying to secure funding, setting up workshops, and brainstorming books and even a website (which, for the time, was particularly forward thinking). He had a wife and a small child and they were trying for another. My mum and he met for lunches and spoke constantly on the phone. And, it seemed, things didn't always remain professional.

One day, in the aftermath, I asked Mum to tell me the truth.

'You dad isn't the same man I married,' she said. And I understood. I thought back to my dolls, the way the sensible thing to do had been to leave when I played that part of the unhappy partner. But now, even the slight possibility that she might abandon my dad deeply unsettled me. I instantly despised her for it.

I never went looking for love with The Scientist. But he began to bandy the word around so freely, about my body mainly, that the adrenaline coursing through me led me to imagine I might just have found it.

Perhaps, after everything, I might deserve it.

The text repartee continued. More unrequited photos and videos from me; emails full of longing. We had both chosen not to tell anyone about our developing relationship, without consulting each other. It made it feel special, like an inside joke that only we knew about. I'd flush when an inappropriate message pinged on my phone at a meeting, but bat away attention by saying I'd just seen something funny on social media.

One day we'd both been invited to the same event by chance and we plotted our union afterwards. The drive to my house was filled with tension. This was it; it was finally going to happen. And I wanted it too.

When we got inside he asked for wine and I had a glass as well, although it was early. I didn't know what to do next and then he made a suggestion.

Minutes later I was standing at the bottom of my stairs, completely naked. He inspected me as though I was livestock at an auction. He liked to describe parts of my body as though analysing them in a laboratory. I went to remove his clothes and he backed away. 'That's not going to happen,' he said. And I couldn't understand why. He was allowed to touch me, but I wasn't allowed to reciprocate. I began to regret this whole thing.

After a few months, the texts and messages became less fraught with desire and more just fraught. We had fallen into something of an uncomfortable rhythm: he'd promise to see me, I would ask him to commit to a date, then something would come up – from illness, to work, or a family issue.

Sometimes he'd call me on the way back from the airport and I foolishly always answered, ever hopeful of a return to the innocent clandestine conversations we'd had in the early weeks of our relationship. Contact with him was like a drug I found difficult to give up. I would back off and desperately try to forget him, only for him to message out of the blue. If I ever called him it went straight to voicemail. He rarely wanted to be seen in public with me. When we did meet, it was always on his terms, and he controlled what took place.

Our relationship went from feeling special to feeling sordid. I liked the fact he was away a lot, that he had his own place and own life. I would settle for something casual. But I was suspicious.

'Are you certain he's not married? Or has kids?' asked my therapist.

'He definitely doesn't have children,' I said. 'And he is definitely not married. Though I do wonder if he's in a relationship.'

As soon as those words had come out of my mouth her body language changed. Her job was, of course, not to judge anything that was said within the confines of a session. But I could see it written all over her face. To her I was 'The Other Woman'.

I am in Scotland on assignment. Temporarily cut off from a strong phone signal and, with it, my exhausting relationship. This time I am based in the south, in Dumfries and Galloway, sent to highlight this often-overlooked area of the country. I find myself in the Isle of Whithorn, one of the most southerly ports in Scotland. I'd only stopped here to try to find a decent cup of coffee and get out from behind the wheel. But I quickly stumble upon a ruin: the remains of a chapel, St Ninian's.

The origins of St Ninian – who is thought to have predated St Columba and the missionary in Iona by over a century – are shrouded in mystery. One of the main sources of historical information about the saints in Britain was written by a man called Bede in the eighth century. The *Ecclesiastical History of the English People* is the most comprehensive document that exists detailing the saints and their followers in Britain. However, Bede seems to have got Ninian and his contemporary Columba confused, leading historians to question other details. What is known, though, is that Ninian was Scottish, lived in the fourth and fifth centuries, and converted a great many Picts to Christianity.

Breaking with popular convention at the time, when Ninian constructed his church here in Dumfries, he eschewed the standard wood-and-clay prototype and instead built it out of stone, whitewashing it to protect it from the elements. He called the building Candida Casa (Latin for 'shining house') and the priory is still white today.

The quayside and St Ninian's ruined chapel were once only connected to the rest of the village via a shingle causeway that would become covered daily with the tides. Now, though, it is permanently open to pedestrian traffic, the only exception being when extremely high spring tides or storms cause it to flood.

I walk up to the roofless shell of the chapel, its corners still strong and holding firm. A huge space for grand windows is now wide open to the sea, and slots where beams were once placed remain as empty notches. This chapel is not the original. It was first built in 1100, then rebuilt again in 1300. But it was a place used as a sanctuary by pilgrims who had journeyed, often over water, to arrive at the shrine of the saint.

Alongside the structure I spy a wind-weathered marker post that describes a walking route set up by a local group called The Whithorn Pilgrim Way. I try to decipher the illustrated map, but it is so scuffed by time and waves that it feels like trying to decode an ancient text penned by Bede himself. Squinting, I can just make out that it appears to go along the coast a little before turning inland and heading up towards Glenluce, a small village distinguished by its impressive array of crumbling canonical buildings –

including the 800-year-old abbey, in which the stained-glass windows of the chapter house are still intact despite the rest of the structure falling into decay.

Somewhere inland the trail looks to perform a loop, but even with my own OS map to compare it with I can't quite make sense of it. Regardless, it would be far too long a trail for me to undertake. I have only two days left here and interviews to complete before I must move on.

I turn away, resigned to the fact that this pilgrimage is not one I will get to tread. Then I spot a sign directing walkers to St Ninian's Cave, just over 8 kilometres away. It is still early and I work out that I can make it and get back in good time for my next appointment. And so, without even my longed-for coffee in hand, I head off on my own micro-pilgrimage from the saint's chapel to the place where it's said he would go to pray and think.

Over the months that have passed since my visit to Iona, I had not given myself any time to enjoy being outside. The pilgrim paths that had been helping me so much had been pushed aside. Instead, I'd filled my time with work once more, determined to account for every single minute. I was lonely, but didn't want to appear to anyone that I was sat around just waiting for my phone to ring, wishing that someone – anyone – wanted to spend time with me.

On the rare occasions when I was too exhausted to work any more, I would try to make sense of my relationship with The Scientist. It was as if I now had become the one engaged in a controlled experiment, analysing data, looking for patterns or clues. I would scroll through the affectionate and refined flirtatious texts we'd exchanged in the early days and try to understand how they had become the blunt – bordering on indifferent – interactions we had now. I started to notice how he would often be demanding, pressing to meet me in London when it suited him, only to pick an argument with me, twisting my attempts to fix a time and place into 'neediness'. And somehow, it was always me who ended up apologising to him, and he would kindly, magnanimously, forgive me.

As I walk, I reflect on all this, away from the distraction of my laptop or a beeping phone. The brackish air is welcome in my lungs, which over the previous months have become choked full of exhaust fumes from cities, in Britain and further afield.

I look back at the chapel. The isle is now a prominent spur of land stretching out into the harbour, and a boat with a red hull bobs on the waves bound for it. It's said that due to this location's proximity to Ireland and the Cumbrian coast, people especially from the north of England and southern Scotland would travel for days if not weeks to get here on pilgrimage. I wonder if any of the pilgrims arrived and were disappointed by what they found. Did they realise that the journey to an unknown goal is infinitely better than reaching it? Did they regret the anticlimactic moment when they discovered their destination was just another building – albeit coated in fancy white décor?

In the depths of Dad's depression everything seemed to disappoint him. He'd always worked a lot when we were kids, but when we did have him to ourselves, he was always the fun one. He would sneak us extra pocket money, let us stay up that bit later, and when we went outdoors he would run and jump and laugh.

But after his diagnosis nothing seemed to give him that same joy. My mum would encourage me to spend time with him, and I always did, but it was hard. As a teenager I was already starting to become world-weary myself, so being with someone who vocalised the same feelings of disgust and disappointment made me feel like everything – life, love, the future – was hopeless.

For a time, though, a little after we united along the North Wales Pilgrim's Way, we drew closer to one another again. Maybe it was because I'd left my partner and job, and shaken up my life to an unrecognisable degree. Dad was also alone. Our relationship was entirely free from any interfering women or conflicting interests.

We suddenly found ourselves as equals. Both hurt from the past. Both single. Both unsure of what would come next. And for a while we bonded in a way I had all but given up on. We laughed and teased each other, I took him with me on some work assignments and watched on like a parent might do as he tried activities he never thought he would. I saw him ride a horse, eat octopus (he always hated seafood), and got to witness the sheer wonder on his face as he went snorkelling for the first time.

One evening, when we were alone, I finally asked him all of the questions I'd bottled up in the years following Mum's death, and about the affair she might have had. Sometimes we could barely make eye contact, but we did, I believe, come to a mutual understanding: that he and my mum were not perfect humans, or perfect partners, and that was okay.

Despite her love of essential oils, her long flowing skirts and dreams of walking barefoot in the Indian Himalaya, my mum adored technology. One of her favourite pastimes was to read everything she could about a new phone, computer or time-saving device before confusing the staff at the local electronics shop with her newly learned lingo, when they mistook her as a clueless housewife.

Before she died, Mum treated herself to a brand-new laptop and made me swear I wouldn't tell my dad. After she died, Dad found an unpaid credit invoice for it hidden amid the pages of a book called *The Games People Play*. It was the first time I saw him laugh after we lost her, and he kept chuckling for hours.

I still have that laptop today, though I've never known its password. The words and truths on her hard drive remain hidden in pixels that I'll never get to decode.

'Do you think she ever did act on that email with her colleague?' I asked Dad.

'I don't know,' he said. 'But if she did, I would have understood. I wasn't the same person after my breakdown. I couldn't provide all I had promised. I was difficult and hard to live with. And she deserved to be happy.'

And in that moment, I was overwhelmed by the love my dad had shown.

The waves crash loudly, echoing in my ears as the visual drama of the expanding Scottish coastline also intensifies. Spoils of the granite cliffs lie in fragments metres below the pathway, sticking out of the churning sea like croutons in a white soup, while broom and bindweed creep between the cracks spooling beyond the edges.

Though the route I am on isn't technically an 'official' pilgrim route, the names along this stretch of coastline point to a biblical past. From 'Devil's Head' to 'Rock of Providence', it is hard to believe that the late saint or his subsequent followers didn't have some hand in christening these landmarks.

At Burro Head there is a small caravan park that reminds me of those peppered along the coast where I grew up. For a second I flash back to Rhyl, Prestatyn and Towyn. I remember Mum once holidayed there as a child, when she was just eleven. Now a modern housing estate, it was once the location of a Derbyshire Miners' Holiday Camp – a place opened so that working-class people could afford to experience the seaside after the Holidays with Pay Act of 1938. Her dad had set aside a portion of his wages every week through the Derbyshire District Colliery Workers' Holiday Savings Scheme, meaning they could go for a few days' break. We still have the photograph of her there, smiling excitedly and cuddling a giant rabbit. The wallpaper is busy and garish behind her blonde curly hair.

I remember her telling me how she became lost on her first and only visit to the beach and got sunburnt. When she was first diagnosed with a melanoma at the age of forty-five, the consultant said it was likely this incident had caused it.

It was here on the Scottish coast where I wander that much of the 1973 film *The Wicker Man* was shot – in particular the final scene, where the policeman, enticed here to investigate the disappearance of a local girl, unwittingly dresses up as a fool and is burned alive in a human effigy.

Beneath the main cliff on which I stand another offshoot of spiky rocks protrudes from beneath the waves, edged by a fringe of green. On it stands a flight of cormorants, their wings outstretched like darkened holy robes, reptilian necks extended as they regard their surrounds with condescending glances.

Watching them, my eyes scan the horizon, and then I see it.

Ahead, the grassy clifftops descend onto a beach, made up of a collection of sand and small pebbles, stretching on for about 500 metres before coming to an abrupt end thanks to a huge chunk of cliff face towering above it. But even over a kilometre away I can see a gaping hole in that cliff – the entrance to my destination: St Ninian's Cave.

When it comes to religion, the role of the hermit is well documented. A hermit is a person who retires from society into the wilderness, to find a place to live in solitude. The first record of such a soul comes from the fourth century, in a book called *Life of Saint Paul the First Hermit*, penned in the year 375 by an early Christian priest called Jerome of Stridon. It talks of a time between 227 and 341 (during which years, at some point, the subject, Paul of Thebes, is said to have lived) when Christians were persecuted in Egypt by the Roman Emperor and had to flee to the desert so that they could keep worshipping their god and live a life of prayer and penance. The idea was to have an austere place, with no home comforts, so that one's full focus could be devotion to the Lord. St Dwynwen chose an island; St Paul is said to have lived in the Theban desert; St Columba, as I'd seen on Iona, went to a stone hut on a lonely shore; and Ninian, it is believed, came to this cave.

In some ways I've spent a lot of my life voluntarily living like a hermit. I was first isolated from friends by coercion, finding it easier to escape accusations of wrongdoing by not having the chance to do anything in the first place. Then when Mum died, I removed myself from social situations by choice to make others feel more comfortable away from my grief. Since The Scientist has appeared in my life, I realise I've started doing it again.

The night before I'd left to come to Scotland I'd been at a writers' event in London and soon the conversation turned to shared acquaintances. I scarcely listened as they discussed a woman I knew a little, but not well.

And then they said it.

She had been living with The Scientist for the last few years and, to their knowledge, still was.

I felt my stomach lurch. It couldn't be right. 'You must be mistaken,' I said. 'Absolutely not,' came the reply.

The conversation continued but all I heard was a distorted din, as though someone had turned down the volume. The room started to blur. I excused myself to use the toilet and promptly ran into an unoccupied cubicle and threw up.

My eyes are firmly fixed on Ninian's Cave. I make my way down to the beach and relish the familiar scratching sound of my feet forcing the pebbles to squeeze and slide past one another. The wind is easing and, other than the occasional lap of the waves as they rush up and down the silt, there is no other sound. The beach is empty; I am quite alone.

The cave sits in a naturally formed cleft in the stone edge of the collapsed headland of Port Castle Bay. Once it would have been an elaborate dwelling place, but erosion has seen it shrink over time. Now, it's just 7 metres long, with a mouth of 3 metres – the same as its entire internal width. Outside, crosses have been carved into the stone by pilgrims from bygone ages. I place my hand over them, trying to read them as though they are braille. If I were to carve one, I wonder, would someone else touch it in a hundred years and think of me?

In the 1880s and 1950s, excavations of the site revealed internal walls, passages and the human remains of an older adult and two children. A total of eighteen medieval stone crosses were found, some cleaved into the walls and others left strewn on the floor, leading some theorists to conclude that this place may have later served as a monastic stone-carving workshop.

I call into the opening and my voice comes echoing back to me. Here, alone with my thoughts, that nagging voice from my Spanish Camino comes back with a vengeance. 'Cheat, cheat, cheat', it repeats on a cycle, this time reminding me that I have become someone's mistress, however unwittingly. The ceaseless shriek of a nearby fulmar bounces off the walls, adding to the orchestra of self-loathing.

To think early on that man had accused *me* of being in a relationship, and that I'd recoiled in horror at the thought of it. I recall that at the start of our affair he'd called me by a different name, then claimed it was a joke. Looking back, he'd slowly and deliberately controlled the way we communicated. First, asserting that my texts were no longer getting through to him, so everything had to be moved to another messaging service. Then he said we needed to switch entirely to email. Then email was problematic, something to do with a deadline he was on for a research project, which meant he couldn't reply.

Standing on the windswept beach, presented with all these memories afresh, I know with great certainty these were all lies that I had chosen to believe.

I have become The Other Woman.

Outside the cave entrance a small sign forbids entry, citing the risk of landslips and rockfall. But I don't care. Here, in the cell that Ninian himself called 'a place of terrible blackness', I scream.

SIX

Easter

At first I think it is the wind. A low constant murmur coming from across the horizon. The water splashes cold against my ankles; my bare feet are already numb from the chill of the air. Curlews call out in that distinctive whistle of theirs, while the scratchy raucous shout of a grey heron completes the tuneless melody.

But then all is still. I stop to listen more closely. It isn't the whipping of the wind I can hear but rather a low, penetrating moan; a ceaseless tormented lament coming from the southern edges of Lindisfarne.

This is the cry of the colony of Atlantic grey seals that live, die and give birth around the islets and sandbars of this Holy Island in Northumberland. Marine biologists tell us that the seals are communicating, their calls enabling mothers to stay connected to their pups, or simply, as one guide once told me, offering the joy of song – the chance to feel part of a choir.

Folklore explains it differently, equating their haunting cries to those of sirens or mermaids who lead sailors to their deaths on shallow rocks. In Scottish mythology they are Selkies: seal-like creatures who shed their skin to walk around on land as beautiful women, leading a great many men to their eventual downfall.

The problem with becoming The Other Woman is that, even if it begins by accident, you soon have to make a decision about whether or not to embrace that status. And, if you do, the label will stick to you stubbornly, like a stain you can't get out.

When I realised the truth of what had been happening, I knew I should have walked away. But somehow, I couldn't. I felt caught in a web of lust, yearning, deceit and pride. I could win this, I told myself. To walk away now, that would be weak, and I wasn't ready to be the victim.

In the months that followed, my contact with The Scientist lessened – in frequency, though not intensity. I confronted him with the information I had and he told me I was mistaken, that she was his ex, but they were still going through the process of separating their lives and home. I knew he was lying. Everything was always a rush, with visits wrapped up in a randomly specific timeframe and spurious reasons given for cutting things short. I let him spin his yarns for me, taking delight in watching him tangle up his excuses. I would nod along, but really I knew that she was coming home soon. The danger, though, seemed to be part of the thrill for him. Later, I found posts on his girlfriend's social media of him enjoying a meal with her posted at the exact time he messaged to say he was looking at my nudes.

I would find myself relieved when he was away. I could breathe more easily. There would be no unexpected messages and no demands that I show more of myself.

Eventually, I told some of my male friends about my predicament, correctly anticipating that their reactions would be less judgemental, more pragmatic. But in some ways it seemed to complicate these relationships. One of them came to see me and ended up staying the night on my sofa bed downstairs after a bit too much to drink. It emerged later he'd told his wife he'd stayed at another guy's house, making it look like we had something to hide when we didn't. I assumed that now I was an established Seductress, he believed that something improper could potentially happen between us.

After years of avoiding special occasions, I finally accepted an invite to a wedding party, only to find I was the only single woman there; all of the guests were accompanied by 'other halves' and clutching their offspring. All the talk was about nappies, breastfeeding and naptime – I felt like an alien species. So I went to get myself a drink and ended up chatting to one of the husbands. Another came over when he saw us laughing and fairly soon there was a small group of us, all talking shop. But one by one, the men were called away and I was left, once more, by myself.

After the solitude I'd experienced at St Ninian's hermit cave I decide my next adventure should not be undertaken alone. Having some company might not cure the way I am feeling, but it might just provide a distraction. It is nearly Easter, the time of year that I've always found the hardest since Mum died. In Britain, Mother's Day is eternally linked to Easter. Originating in the Middle Ages, it is always the fourth Sunday in Lent (a period of fasting echoing Jesus' time in the desert). That was when worshippers would traditionally return to their 'Mother Church', the church where they were baptised.

I soon stumble across a group called Northern Cross, who describe themselves as 'ordinary Christians' and each year walk a route to Holy Island, Lindisfarne, carrying a wooden cross between them as a team, before spending Easter on the isle in a vigil. It began in the 1970s when a few pilgrims took part in another, larger, group walk, then known as Student Cross, which saw an annual Easter Walk from London to Walsingham Abbey in Norfolk. Northern Cross decided they wanted to walk elsewhere and, with the idea to walk between the borders of England and Scotland on a number of different routes, hit upon Lindisfarne as their final destination. This walk, however, has already left without me.

Nearer to me in Oxfordshire is the St Birinus Pilgrimage, which at the time happened annually, beginning in the small Thameside village of Dorchester before making its way across the chalk downs for sixteen kilometres to a tumulus known as Churn Knob, the site where the eponymous saint had converted the King of Wessex from paganism to Christianity in 635 AD. The conversion seems to have been a strategic political move to persuade Oswald, the King of Northumbria, to ally with him to defeat the Mercians (who lived in the area now known as The Midlands).

All roads seem to lead back to Northumberland. So I refocus my attention there and come across Trail Outlaws, started by an IT consultant turned event-organiser from Blackpool called Tim Bateson. While recceing new routes for his ultra-marathon races, running one day above Wooler, a small town just beyond the border of Northumberland National Park, he noticed signs for the St Cuthbert's Way.

Founded in 1996, this 100-kilometre trail begins at the abbey in the Scottish border town of Melrose, where the saint is believed to have started his religious journey. The route crosses between the multi-pronged mass of the

Eildon Hills and over the lonely rounded bumps of the Cheviots, following river bends and emerging from woodlands to end at the Holy Island where Cuthbert was originally buried.

'I'm not religious, but I was raised Catholic,' says Tim, when I call him to ask why he's chosen a pilgrim path for a race course. He almost whispers it, as though confessing to a priest. 'It was already an established path, and easy to follow for participants, so it did make sense,' he adds.

In 2015, Tim first ran his event on the St Cuthbert's Way starting from Lindisfarne and ending in Melrose, but in recent years he'd decided to switch the route direction to make it even more of a challenge. Rebranded as the 'Race Against the Tide', the Ultra's strict cut-off points for participation are timed with the twice-daily tides that see Holy Island completely cut off from the mainland. During those periods, the causeway – which is large enough to take cars in both directions as well as pedestrians – is completely flooded. Now it was mother nature, rather than marshals, who dictated whether or not competitors could finish the race.

'For most people it's a personal challenge, though there are definitely some who come to win it and others who are attracted to the route,' he explains. 'To those who have never run an Ultra it sounds insane, but then it's like a pilgrimage really – a mental challenge more than anything.

In the end it's not your body that decides whether or not you can go on, it's your mind.' Trail running, Tim tells me, also has a meditative quality: the semi-technical routes of uneven terrains means you have to be in the present – not worried about yesterday or tomorrow, just focused on each movement.

Tim has other routes in his sights. One is the 'Way of Light' he found on the British Pilgrimage Trust's website, which runs from the site of the Battle of Heavenfield, near Hexham – where King (soon to be Saint) Oswald would record a victory that marked the putative dawn of Christianity in Britain – to Durham Cathedral, the shrine where St Cuthbert would eventually be laid to rest. The other, he tells me, is the Camino.

He reveals that he had been married for twenty years and began to worry that it wasn't working out. So he decided to walk the pilgrim path to rediscover himself. He had everything booked and ready to go, but then his father fell ill and he cancelled it. His dad died just weeks later, when he would have been walking on the Camino and uncontactable. He says he is glad and relieved he decided to change his plan.

'I was physically ready to do it back then, but not mentally,' he says. 'I was overly cocky. But now, after choosing to end my marriage and losing my dad, I think I will get more out of it, spiritually.'

Tim planned to finally run the Camino the next year, so he'd be there for what would have been his dad's birthday in April.

St Cuthbert is a popular figurehead for the Church in the north-east. During his life he is said to have saved a raft of monks from Iona who were headed to Holy Island before he had even taken vows himself. He was seemingly blessed with privileged visions – once writing of witnessing a figure descending from the sky amid a beam of light to collect the body of Aidan, the man in whose footsteps he would later follow at both Melrose Abbey and Lindisfarne. While he was undertaking his training, a change was afoot in the Church. Leaders of the diocese at Whitby, under whose jurisdiction Northumbria then fell, decided that they should no longer be looking to the Irish for their religious guidance. The monks, who had laboured under the teachings of Columba, returned to the Scottish island, leaving spaces for locals in Lindisfarne, where Cuthbert was then posted.

After ten years, in 676 AD, Cuthbert sought the life of a hermit and took himself over to Inner Farne, south of the Holy Island, to enjoy a life of solitude and prayer. It was not to be. Visitors keen to seek his wisdom were frequent, so much so that he built a guesthouse (called the Fishehouse), the ruins of which can still be seen by the landing jetty. He constructed a small chapel and a cell, and was renowned for caring for the sea birds that shared the island with him, thereby becoming one of the earliest known conservationists. Even now the eider is known in these parts as a Cuddy duck – a shortened name for Cuthbert.

However, in 684 his retirement was disturbed permanently when he was made Bishop of Lindisfarne and called back to serve others again. Nowadays the Farne Islands are a National Nature Reserve, where puffins, razorbills, guillemots, terns and, of course, his beloved eider ducks come to nest, all under the protection of a different kind of entity – the National Trust.

Cuthbert died in 687 and his body was enshrined on Lindisfarne for nearly two hundred years, making the place something of a pilgrim destination.

Despite my desire for company, I set off to do a section of this route alone, hopeful I'll find some peace on Cuthbert's Holy Island.

I head east in my car, on the lonely road to Haltwhistle, from Carlisle, where I'd just given a talk to a room full of strangers. As my vehicle moves forwards, the wind and rain seem to push it back. It isn't yet night-time, but the sky has become so dark from the growing storm that I have to squint through the windscreen just to see the white lines on the road.

A couple of days earlier, back home, I'd received an urgent message from The Scientist: 'I have a hotel booked in Central London for work – come see me.' The last time he'd done this, he'd unceremoniously changed his mind at the last minute and then made me apologise for being too clingy. So I was cautious about coming on too strong, breezily agreeing before going about my day.

I purposely arranged a full day of meetings so that if the plans with him fell apart I wouldn't feel foolish. All the meetings I had were booked in and diarised; no one was going to let me down. The last engagement was a book launch for a friend. There was wine to drink and intelligent people to chat to about the world, and I forgot about our plans.

A message pulled me back in: I should meet him in forty-five minutes. Typical short notice. I said I would do my best, but then got chatting to someone else, and by the time I realised that half an hour had passed I had to run to grab a taxi rather than the tube.

'You'll need to go straight to the lift when you arrive – it's by reception to the left. If you're asked, say "we" have a room and I'm already here ...' came the instruction. In the past I would have felt special to read this, like a spy in a movie: undercover, surreptitious. But I felt different now;

irked, a little insulted by the quotation marks around the word 'we'.

The traffic was awful, I was very late, and as I stepped out of the taxi and the fresh air hit me, I felt tipsy. Part of me was worried I might cause a scene. Part of me hoped I would.

No one asked who I was or why I was there when I made my way into the lobby and strode boldly towards the lift. It had been a while since we'd met last, with very few exchanges in between. The conversation was stilted. It was late. I was tired and the room was swaying. It felt as though we were on a ship together. I was worried about the time. I told him so. Then our usual ritual began.

Afterwards, I noticed the clock, realising I would certainly miss my last train.

When he asked what time it left the station and I told him in ten minutes – so no chance – within seconds he had forced my coat on me and bundled me towards the door. Wishing me good luck, he slammed it behind me, leaving me alone in the corridor.

I didn't make the train that night. Instead, I spent several hours cold and shivering, being harassed by homeless people for cash, which I gladly gave as a way of penance for my stupidity, waiting for the pre-dawn service to deliver me home on this extended walk of shame.

He never checked to see if I had made it back safely. It was the last time we met.

I decide I will walk to Lindisfarne in a single day, followed by a wild camp once I return to the mainland. When I'd spoken to Tim he'd said of his run from Wooler to the coast that there's 'no one from you to the horizon'. It sounded like the perfect beginning.

Before I'd left for the north, a colleague had presented me, unexpectedly, with an Easter egg. He had expressed concern over the last few months that I wasn't eating and said he was worried I was wasting away. I had left it on the passenger seat of my car, planning to throw it away when I stopped. Food, after all, was something I could still control. But just in case, on the off-chance I couldn't find anything to eat on my journey, I put it in my backpack.

I leave the town and follow the metalled trail up a steep hill, before it becomes a grass track around Weetwood Moor. The bracken stands to attention like centurions, towering over the route ahead. Behind me the Cheviots roll into the distance, tantalising me with swathes of the rest of the route I've missed. Ahead is farmland and myriad pockets of wooded copses.

After Cuthbert died, back on his chosen Inner Farne, his body was returned to Lindisfarne and buried in the church in a stone coffin. Hearing of his devotion to God, people would come to pay their respects at his

184

headstone and, little by little, they began to report miracles.

Back in those days it wasn't enough for people to simply visit a marker in a cemetery, or gaze at a plaque in the floor of a church. It was, as was seen with Saint James in Spain, all about the relics – the remains of a deceased holy man. A plan of action was decided upon by the monks: they would keep him in the coffin for just over a decade, eleven years in fact, so that his body would have time to turn to bones, and then they would exhume it and declare him 'elevated' to sainthood.

When the day finally came in 698 AD, they opened the coffin to find that his entire body remained completely intact with no sign of decomposition. This confirmed his saintly status even more solidly than the miracles, and now crowds of pilgrims came to see his coffin for the next handful of decades. Then, in 793, some unwelcome visitors, uninterested in bodies or saints, made their way to Lindisfarne: the Vikings.

This was not a coincidence. The Vikings were well known for their raids on religious sites. Given the practice of the rich (and the poor) giving money to monks and bishops as payment for their own sins, it was a calculated attack to enable them to claim gold and silver from pacifists who would not fight them for it. In short, it was an attack on the vulnerable.

When they departed Lindisfarne, the Vikings not only left a pile of bodies in their wake and took the younger members of the order to be sold as slaves; they also left the monastery in flames.

The actions of my previous night in London spin through my head like wool on a loom, while quivering skylarks seek to distract me with their alarm call as I unwittingly pass close to their nests on the ground.

Miraculously, the Vikings did not manage to destroy St Cuthbert's body, but the threat still very much remained of another Danish invasion. So a decision was made, in 875, that saw a band of monks leave the priory to carry his (by all accounts) still-uncorrupted body around the countryside for a total of seven years. One of the places they are said to have hidden it is now known as St Cuthbert's Cave.

I find it just off the path in the Kyloe Hills surrounded by forest. A naturally formed rock shelter, it is constructed from an overhanging outcrop of sandstone. The walls that make up its sides are swirled pink and white, stained green by the surrounding foliage. It certainly feels a befitting place for the body of a man who chose to commune with nature and protect birds rather than sit in a study and count his gold.

Here I stay for longer than I had planned, running scenarios in my head as though masterminding a military retreat, unable to quite believe I've allowed myself to go from one bad relationship into another – to escape from a lifetime of feeling controlled to permitting myself the fool-hardy belief anything had changed.

I notice the time and get up, my pace quickening. The tide will not wait.

When finally I stand at the start of the causeway, the seas have parted and the road holds just a slither of water. Until the 1950s the only way to get across to Lindisfarne was over the sand. Visitors nowadays can come via vehicle, but I want to do what all the pilgrims before me have done for centuries – walk across the silt.

It's a 5-kilometre undertaking, the route marked with tall, wooden poles with two platforms – called refuges – in the middle, in case a walker makes a misstep with their tidal planning. Some choose to walk it in wellies but I want to feel the cold water around my feet.

I pull off my boots and socks and tie them methodically to my backpack. Then I press my bare feet into the wet mix of mud and sand, and breathe deeply as I feel the earth squish between my toes. I begin on my way.

The water is spilled into puddles across the mudflats – some large, some tiny. The sun is hidden behind a mackerel sky of cirrocumulus cloudlets, which appear to also be spread out on the ground as though painted on the surface of the standing water. The reflections make the poles that mark the route appear double their already impressive size.

Sometimes a shell cracks underneath my sole, causing me to wince, but I don't stop.

This section of the coast is a constantly changing mix of dunes, mudflats and saltmarsh. It has been shifting over a millennium and doubtlessly looks very different now to how it would have done in the time when the saints and legends were born. Common cordgrass edges the intertidal mud, while the marsh thrives with thrift and briny sea purslane, a favourite of foraging chefs. Eel grass winds its way around my ankles. The water sometimes splashes my exposed calves with muddy spray, but I continue walking, wearing the marks of dirt like a badge of honour that confirms my pilgrim credentials.

I don't have much time to tour the island when I reach solid ground. So, after drying my feet on a clump of marram grass, I leave my backpack on the sand and make my way to the priory with wet feet.

The ravages of civil war and Reformation mean that all that still stands at the site of the 'Cradle of Christianity' are crumbling red walls and gothic-style arches, along with a collection of Celtic crosses, and a trough said to be the site of the shrine where the saint was once lain.

Next to it, the more recently built church of St Mary the Virgin holds inside a list of all the bishops, priors and vicars of Lindisfarne, as well as a sculpture, hewn from seven elm trees, depicting the monks carrying St Cuthbert's coffin to safety. A bronze version stands in the city of Durham, where his remains are still safely entombed.

I leave the church and look out to the island's iconic castle. Built in 1549, it was originally used as a garrison during the civil wars – strategically placed as it was on the borderlands of England and Scotland. Later, in the early 1900s, this former fort became an Edwardian holiday home. It was here that the owner of *Country Life* magazine entertained guests including the author of *Peter Pan*, J. M. Barrie, the First World War's most famous poet, Siegfried Sassoon, and King Edward VIII (then Prince of Wales). It looks every bit the romantic castle, but this is a place where blood was spilled countless times and miracles made mere mortals morph seamlessly into saints.

As I wander back to the beach to collect my bag and start my journey home, my phone rings. I nearly don't answer it, feeling far removed from the rest of the world physically. When I do pick up, it is a company that I am about to sign a contract with to undertake several months of guaranteed work. Everything had been going well but now, they regret to inform me, they've decided to go with someone else: The Scientist's girlfriend – and on his recommendation.

I had been lied to, deceived and made to feel like a fool. I'd been abandoned in the cold and ceaselessly humiliated. But until now, this had all happened in secret. Suddenly, though, my personal and professional lives have collided – and with catastrophic and damaging results, destroying a much-needed work contract and, even worse, potentially ruining my reputation.

Tears sting my eyes as I make my way back towards the mainland. What had taken nearly two hours before, now races by in a matter of minutes. I begin to run, fast, fervently and fuming.

I stop at the first refuge and climb its rickety ladder all the way to the top. There is no roof on these emergency structures, they were not designed for comfort; the authorities don't want to entice a person to willingly become stranded. Yet here I collapse – a wreck, seeking some kind of sanctuary – and howl.

After a long time lying down on the salty wooden slats, I notice the water is beginning to turn again. The tide is coming in and I need to get down and take myself back to land. I step slowly down to the quickening ground and, in spite of myself, keep going.

It is then that I hear the call of the seals and feel a guttural companionship with the creatures who sing to the sea. I had longed for company on this pilgrimage and perhaps, in one way, I have found it.

Beside my feet a single, small periwinkle, its shell turned black by the incoming water, is making its way towards higher ground. Its trail is as deep as mine, though it is moving much more slowly. Against all the odds, it will keep on moving. And I have to as well.

The water has risen to nearly knee height when I reach the mainland and feel solid ground beneath my feet. I take a deep breath and wander along the shoreline. No longer in the realm of the ancient, I am back in the present.

All along I'd stayed committed and loyal to this troubled relationship. I'd been clinging to it as part of my plan to change the path of my life. But, while I had done it to change my route entirely, it seems The Scientist only wanted a brief diversion from his.

I sit on the soft ground and take off my backpack again. I put on my socks and shoes, then reach further into my bag to locate the indulgent chocolate egg given to me by my colleague.

Amid the fuzz in my head, against the shock of my newfound reality, I realise that a line has been crossed and there is no going back. I unwrap the chocolate and begin to eat it, not stopping until I have finished every last piece.

SEVEN

Finisterre

I stand on the edge of an earthen platform and listen to the high-pitched call of a corn bunting that seems to sing a melody just for me. Water and mudflats dominate the horizon, but man's impact on this landscape is evidenced everywhere.

To one side, the huge arms of at least a dozen windmills stand motionless, while their skeletal forms are reflected into perfectly dug dykes. To the other, beyond the outfalls and winding creeks, a collection of Thames barges sit offshore in the North Sea. They were filled with concrete and scuttled in the 1980s, forming a breakwater to protect this vital brackish saltmarsh. Even the grassy bank on which I stand is built by humans, raised high to protect the farmland from the ever-encroaching tide.

The air is filled with the smell of decaying cabbages and swarms with flies. The red legs of a wading oystercatcher seem brazen amid the otherwise muted tones of corn yellow and marsh green. In front of me, in the distance, I can see a lonely church.

There's a rockbound peninsula on the west coast of Galicia that was once believed to be the very western tip of the European continent and, therefore, the end of the Earth. Its Spanish name, which means just that, is Finisterre. Most pilgrims who walk the Camino don't get to it, choosing instead to stop at the cathedral in Santiago and watch the Botafumeiro swing as their finale. Arguably, though, reaching the sea should be the true conclusion. It was here, after all, that the remains of St James are believed to have first come ashore, the catalyst that started the whole pilgrimage tradition in that region of Spain.

Having grown up by the sea, I always feel that when I stand on the shore and watch the waves crash in front of me, I am looking out into oblivion. When we were kids and the sea was rough and the weather torrid, my mum would take us to the promenade in her car and park right in front of the sea wall. We would watch in glee as the waves breached the manmade boundaries and rose like towers above our tiny 2CV before crashing down all around us. As we got older my brother asked not to come, but I urged Mum to go back and squealed in delight every time the waves engulfed our vehicle. Mum mentioned it to someone at work once, who told her it was irresponsible and dangerous, so she felt obliged to stop. But I couldn't stay away.

When I was a teen and some kind of ending was in sight – be it a friendship, a relationship, a parting, I would sneak out of the house when everyone had gone to bed and walk down to the sea to become lost in the thunderous sounds of the ocean.

One of the most distinct aspects of most Western cultures (particularly the British and American) is our inability to talk about endings. We can be scientific about so many things, we have started to talk openly about birth, we've got better at discussing difficult and traumatic experiences, but death, 'the end of things', despite being the greatest certainty, remains the last taboo.

I've never liked goodbyes of any kind. They make me feel awkward. The sudden gush of potentially uncontrollable emotions makes me uncomfortable. I can feel my limbs flailing around, unsure of where they should be. I think that might be why I grabbed my mum's hand as she took her last breath, seeking a physical anchor to see me through the coming storm.

It was only when I went to see my granny in her final hours that I think I finally managed to get a farewell right. Years before she died, when I was fifteen, she'd had a major stroke, leaving her left arm paralysed. Determined to remain self-reliant, she bought an ulu – a curved multipurpose knife traditionally used by Inuit, Iñupiat, Yupik and Aleut women in the Arctic – so that she wouldn't have to rely on someone cutting up her food for her. She would carry it in her handbag and whip it out at restaurants to surprise and sometimes scare the waiting staff. She continued to travel, mainly on boats or ships, so that she could learn new things and see new places, even if she couldn't walk far. And she volunteered for a stroke charity, helping to teach other survivors of the condition to learn to read again. One day, when I was in my late twenties, she called me in tears. The charity had told her she was no longer capable of helping others, and she was devastated. She felt useless and incapable. I believe that was the day she gave up on life.

Soon, her mind began to wander, and she seemed to prefer dwelling in the past than looking to a future she no longer felt anyone wanted her to be a part of. She began to need around-the-clock help. When she was moved into the care home, she deteriorated quickly. The doctor diagnosed her as having had multiple mini-strokes, each one killing off a cluster of brain cells, and each time taking a part of her memory with it. In the weeks before she died, I'd made a book of old photos of our family and took it to show her. When she saw a photo of my mum and dad she thought I was my mum. When I showed her pictures of me she didn't know who I was.

Then came the day I was in south Snowdonia on assignment, wild camping on the shores of the lake known as Llyn Cau, below Cadair Idris. I got a call from Dad telling me that Granny had days left to live – if that. She'd refused to eat or drink and then somehow fallen out of bed during the night and broken her hip. She was too weak for any surgery. The doctor explained that, really, there was no reason she should be dying, but she had simply given up.

I lay there in my small tent while the wind whistled outside. A raven cried out and the poles of my tent shook violently. The doctor was wrong. She hadn't given up, I decided; she had chosen to end it, on her own terms. When I went to see her the next morning my uncle was there; he'd flown over from his home in Thailand, and he told me she hadn't moved or made any attempt at conversation for hours. I sat down on her bed. She was so tiny now it made me feel like I was a mother tucking a child in to sleep.

Rather than tears or apologies or any of the things we are led to believe we should say to someone at their end, I instead began to describe the mountain I'd just come from. I talked of an explosion, the volcanic origins of this land, once created by lava as it poured under the sea and was shaped by the tide into bulbous pillows. I recalled sweeping glaciers that in the last Ice Age had scoured into it great crevices and gaping holes that would become the lake by which I had slept. I recounted the legend of Idris Gawr, a giant who is said to sit on a throne of rock to survey his kingdom. She turned over to look at me but struggled to open her eyes. She reached out to take my hand and I told her it was okay. She didn't need to look at me; she could rest now. One day we would go to that mountain, I said, and stand on its slopes, and she would see for herself just how beautiful it is.

She died hours after my visit.

I later learned that the historical namesake of the giant on Cadair Idris – Idris ap Gwyddno – was a real Welshman thought to have been killed in battle by Oswald of Northumbria, the man who gifted the island of Lindisfarne to St Cuthbert's predecessor.

In religious texts, the 'end of the earth' is usually meant to mean the 'end of man's domain'. And it's a familiar locale around the world, in different cultures and through different ages. In New Zealand, Te Rerenga Wairua, also known as Cape Reinga, at the north-west tip of the Aupōuri Peninsula, is believed by the Māori to be 'the leaping-off place of spirits', and Reinga itself translates as 'underworld'

– the final place where all the deceased go. In Russian Siberia, the Yamal Peninsula, far in the northern reaches of the Arctic, is so called because it is the 'end of the land'. It is home to the Nenets (or Samoyed) people, who have for centuries traditionally herded reindeer, but their way of life is threatened by the exploitation of natural gas reserves. The Canary Island of El Hierro, or the Isla del Meridiano, was thought to be the end of the world by Columbus before he discovered the Americas.

Nowadays, the ends of the earth tends to mean a really long way.

I'd figuratively felt like I'd reached the end of my own world on several occasions, but my mum's death is the one to which I return emotionally whenever another relationship dies.

· Though the day of her death was hard, and the funeral difficult, for me it was what followed that was much worse. Because, whether it be after the death of a loved one, or the end of a relationship, there's always someone left behind. After Mum was gone, I felt the pressure to continue on immediately with my life, to try to pretend all was the same as it was before. People were more comfortable with that.

Once the responsibility of arranging the funeral and scattering the ashes had passed, I was left feeling empty, numb and pointless. It took years to understand that I had not allowed myself any time to process what had happened.

It was like losing a limb and then wondering why you keep stumbling.

The same is true of relationships, I think.

After my affair with The Scientist ended I was left feeling undone. The stable aspect of my life, the safety net – my work – had also been ripped out from under me. I felt erratic. I made bad decisions and questioned the remaining good ones.

I tried to throw myself back into the same pattern as before, working until I fell asleep at my keyboard, going out running late at night when I tended to feel at my lowest, all in an attempt to keep negative thoughts behind me. But everything felt pointless and shallow. I began to feel as hopeless as I had when I went to the woods that evening thinking I would never return.

There was one person, though, who wouldn't let me give up. A male friend, who everyone called Jack. We'd met a couple of years before, by chance, when we'd been inadvertently connected through work. He was married with children, and as he lived a long way away we'd kept in touch, as many friends do, via occasional funny emails or messages. But when we did manage to get together we acted like a pair of giddy teenagers. Both passionate about wildlife and landscapes, we sometimes managed to squeeze in wild camps, hell-bent on pointless missions such as finding a hidden landmark, or spotting a rare animal. It felt like a true friendship, one that seemed to run so deep it was as though we'd known each other for a time much longer than we'd both been alive.

When things with The Scientist imploded, and I began to shut myself off from anyone and everyone, despite the physical distance between us Jack was one of the few people who noticed my withdrawal. His supportive words got me through. He said: 'You are not like everyone else. You have, for years, been creating a path that wasn't already laid out for you to follow. Breaking trail is exhausting. It's okay to find it hard.'

His words reminded me of hiking alone in winter. Unlike in summer where all the footpaths are easy to see, under snow they are erased. You suddenly have to read the landscape alongside a map to ensure you stay safe. Not only does it tax you mentally, but each footstep is difficult. Without anyone else's bootprints to follow, you often sink deep into the snow up to your knees, then pull your leg out and have to do it all over again, with the remaining strength you can summon. Going uphill literally involves taking one step forward and two steps back. Yet when you do find the power to do it, and you do reach the top of that mountain, every single step you've taken seems worthwhile.

When I first told Jack about The Scientist he berated me for not telling him sooner. He couldn't understand why I'd been carrying this burden alone for so long. I told him

I was worried that if I had mentioned it he would think differently of me and it would change the relationship we had. Who, after all, would want to be friends with The Other Woman?

One night when we met for a drink in a pub, he told me I needed to put myself out there, that I was special, that I was deserving of love. I cried into my beer and told him I wasn't.

But, with Jack's support, I dragged myself out of bed and set about finding a new pilgrim path to tread. My requirement was that it be far from any crowds. I wanted to be a hermit once more. I looked this time to the south-east, to an area I'd read about but never had a reason to venture to before: Essex.

Despite its long-standing stereotypes, this county is actually home to some of the most intriguing natural landscapes in Britain. It has a coastline that traces a distance that's further than London is from Paris. It is home to thirty-five islands and a huge stretch of wetlands and salt-marshes that is designated as being of international importance. It's also home to one of the most isolated religious sites in Britain. And there's a pilgrim trail that runs right to it.

The St Peter's Way is a relatively new venture. It was first proposed in 1978 by two members of the local West Essex Ramblers group, Fred Matthews and Harry Bitten, who were keen to protect the countryside from overdevelopment and showcase the wild and beautiful parts of their county.

Spanning sixty-six kilometres, it was officially adopted by Essex County Council in 2011 when they produced a guide to the route, and the year I walk it, new waymarkers have been put up due to the ever-growing popularity of pilgrim paths.

It starts in the tiny town of Chipping Ongar, a settlement on the convergence of several old roads, home to a church whose priest famously perished on the *Titanic*, refusing to leave so that he could pray with those having to stay behind. It's also near a wooden church called St Andrew's, in Greensted, thought to be the oldest of its kind in the world.

The path's terminus is found at the end of Essex, at an easternmost extremity of Bradwell called the Dengie Peninsula, where there sits an isolated church called St Peter's-on-the-Wall. There's no clear reason the route follows the path that it does, other than it utilises existing footpaths and takes in some of the region's most picturesque scenery.

I begin at Ongar on a sunny day and am almost immediately blinded looking up at the silhouetted cross formed by the weathervane on top of St Martin's Church. It is warm for spring and I am already thirsty.

The path takes me through verdant crops of wheat, aligned geometrically and perfectly uniform, so that they cease to appear natural. Footbridges lead me over the River Roding, which will eventually merge with the Thames at Barking in Greater London. Signs seal off fields to me, declaring themselves as private land.

Being out in Essex so far from all the events of the previous month feels like a tonic I didn't know I needed. I thought I'd spend the days on the trail endlessly dissecting events from my toxic past and torturing myself by replaying key scenes over and over in my head, wishing I could do things differently. But I barely think about The Scientist at all.

And this isn't a work assignment either. This is something new for me. I am throwing myself into a walk just because I want to. I discover an old bypass at the village of Blackmore, constructed during the Plague in 1349 because the disease had killed so many residents that they decided to divert travellers away from their community to help halt the spread of this devastating infection.

I notice bullet holes in the roof of the Church of St Lawrence, the remnants of shots fired in the seventeenth century during the English Civil War when the Parliamentarians fought the Royalists over the right to religious freedom.

Between hawthorn branches I spy a herd of fallow deer watching me, watching them. And outside the hamlet of Margaretting I find a hidden grove filled with bluebells.

For my overnight accommodation I have booked Airbnbs, wanting the privacy of being alone, and removing the need to carry a huge backpack or worry about finding a secluded camping spot.

On the second day, I gaze up at old windmills and a new radar station punctuated with arable fields filled with sprouting broad beans. I edge Hanningfield Reservoir. This body of water was built in 1951 by flooding a hamlet called Peasdown, which mainly consisted of an old stone manor, whose bricks were then used to construct the dam.

My only walking companions are those who call this place home – the flash of white from a brimstone butterfly, or the reassuring knock of a green woodpecker on a nearby tree. The soundtrack is the steady crunch of my boots as they connect with the trail.

At Purleigh, the crops switch from grains to grapes as I reach the site of one of the oldest wine producers in England. Mundon affords me glimpses of St Mary's Church through mesh fencing. Dutifully maintained by the spirit-liftingly named 'Friends of the Friendless' (an organisation that rescues dilapidated religious buildings from ruin to preserve them for everyone's enjoyment), it's made of wood and covered with a clay skirt. A signpost says this building inspired H. G. Wells to pen *War of the Worlds*. It is sealed off for repairs when I am there, but there are no workers I can see, making it feel like I'm strolling through a movie set curiously abandoned in the middle of a shoot.

The highlight comes at the field of 'petrified oaks', which are neither petrified, nor all oaks. It is an incredibly haunting sight, though. The field contains around half a dozen dead oak and ash species, thought to have once been part of a great forest that stood here and that was used by boatbuilders to make vessels for the Royal fleet. Now they stand, frozen in time, their once great branches twisted and leafless, reaching out to hold a hand that will never be offered to them. They are fenced off from the footpath, with a scattering of signs that say 'keep out' and warn that CCTV is watching. It feels somehow apocalyptic. I stand for several minutes, rooted to the spot like they are, watching and waiting.

Further on, I gain my first sight of Maylandsea and the Maldon Marshes. Here, a medieval practice of marsh grazing once saw borrow dykes, sea walls, wet flushes and pools formed as humans attempted to control the tides and claim land back from the sea. From the banks it looks like a winding river with the odd pocket of brackish ditches, but to the flocks of wading birds who perform acrobatics in the skies above, the whole place is a complex jigsaw of land and water.

The route I am following doesn't just take pilgrims straight to the church at the end, but, rather, seems to revel in building up anticipation, revealing the religious finale only from the earthen sea wall, by which time the ends of the Essex earth have already been reached.

It's only when I climb this manmade platform on my final day, and look over to the church, that I begin to reclaim my thoughts away from the trail.

I feel sorrow for what I have lost with The Scientist, but I also feel an incredible sense of relief that it is all over. Throughout the secrecy and the deception, the aspect far worse than the relationship ending was not knowing if it ever would.

In the aftermath of the break-up, before I journeyed to Essex, I had travelled to Northern Ireland, the other extremity of my country, to meet two former nuns who had encountered adversity of their own. Martina Purdy and Elaine Kelly had decided, in 2014, to end their lives as a BBC political correspondent and family lawyer respectively, and start new ones, as nuns in the Christian community of the Adoration Sisters.

When I met them, they had not long been turfed out of their convent before they could take their final vows. 'We were stripped of our habits, congregation, way of life and home in a single moment,' Martina told me. The reason for their expulsion was dwindling congregation numbers, which, the pair were informed, were below what was sustainable for the Catholic Church.

When it looked like all hope was lost for a future that they had given up so much to pursue, they found solace not within the pews of a church, but outside, while walking on the Lecale Coast, in Northern Ireland's far east.

Here the landscape of waves, beach and rock was somehow reassuring. And while they studied maps and worked out the best sections to tread, they realised that they had been following an old pilgrimage route themselves – that of St Patrick, Ireland's patron saint and predecessor to Saints Columba and Cuthbert.

Though the signposts on the ground now describe the footpath as the Lecale Way, Elaine showed me an old map that had St Patrick's Way denoted on several trails in the area that seemed to peter out and disappear. Colloquially, it seemed this was the old 'Pilgrim Way' and it made sense. It traced the coast from the edge of Strangford Lough, where Patrick is said to have landed in Ireland on his return to the country (he is believed to have been a Welsh or English Roman slave who was sold to an owner in Ireland, only to find God and manage to escape back to Britain) to unite the Celtic pagans through Christianity.

In walking the broken clifftops, contemplating their faith amid the wildflowers and watching gannets dive for fish out at sea, Martina and Elaine also found something else – the ancient holy well where it's said Patrick baptised his converts.

The discovery led to the women declaring this to be Ireland's Coastal Camino, and they went on to guide walkers along these pathways to help them find their way, too – even helping doctors and nurses escape the hospital stress during lockdown when Covid hit, a year later.

For both of them the walking, the pilgrimage, the time and space were the cure for a loss of direction that had nearly cost them their faith.

The saltmarshes in Essex have, like the congregations in churches such as Elaine and Martina's, been in slow decline for many years. Biblical-sounding rising seas and an increase in the frequency and severity of storms have caused their gradual loss. Unless you're a birdwatcher or conservationist, you might not think these landscapes are anything more than long and unattractive stretches of mud that are impossible to walk on. Indeed, they were once regarded as 'wasteland'. But they are vital ecosystems that not only help prevent flooding but also support wildlife, including fish, birds and rare plants. They also sequester carbon at a rate ten times faster than mature, tropical forests. In short, they may not appear to be worth saving, but that doesn't mean they shouldn't be protected.

I walk the last steps to St Peter's church, named after one of Jesus' original apostles who, it's said, somehow made it over here and sat upon the wall of the Roman fort that once stood in its place.

I arrive on foot, but the man who founded it, Cedd, came by boat. He was an understudy of St Cuthbert and well respected for his communication skills – it's said he could interpret several languages (vital in Britain in the seventh century when there was a heady mix of Old English, Welsh, Irish and Latin widely spoken) and so in 654 AD he was sent here from Lindisfarne to help convert the East Saxons to Christianity.

When he landed at Bradwell and found the spot where the church sits today, referenced in Bede's *Historia Ecclesiastica* as 'Ythanceaster', he had intended to build it out of wood, as was most common at the time. But the opportunity to use the spoils of the old fortification (one of nine constructed by the Romans to protect against invasion from the Saxons) proved too tempting, so it was built out of stone on top of the old fort's former gateway.

On my way to it I pass a bloom of bindweed, a white and pink circular flower that is also known as 'Our Lady's Little Glass' as it was said to have been used by the Virgin

Mary as a vessel from which to drink wine when she helped a wagoner remove his cart from the mud. I look out to the mudflats and cocklespits where redshank and ringed plover pick through the crustaceans in the hope of finding food.

From the outside, the stone building looks like a barn, and in fact that's how it managed to escape the destruction that befell most other religious buildings during the Reformation. Locals here converted it into a shelter for cattle, cutting a huge entryway into its sidewall to allow the cows to easily enter. In 1916, the family who owned it gave it to the cathedral in Chelmsford and by 1920 the animal entrance was bricked up and the building reconsecrated so that it could serve as a church once more.

I can still make out the old cattle doorway, which appears as an archway of brighter yellow bricks amid more weathered stones. The roof is made from orange tiles that help stop it from merging into the surrounds.

I step inside to find a large but simple single room, the ceiling held up by huge exposed timber beams, and, across the floor, uncomplicated wooden benches are offered as pews. The only splash of colour comes from a red cross depicting Jesus at his crucifixion, with a kneeling figure in blue on one side and a red one on the other. Beneath it lies an undecorated small altar made of stone.

When the church was first reopened they used a wooden altar made from old oak beams from Chelmsford

Cathedral. But in 1980 this one was built from a trio of stone taken from Iona, Lindisfarne and Lastingham, the latter being Cedd's last posting. It seems that no matter where I go on my pilgrimages, all roads end up leading back to one another. Pathways and people link unexpectedly.

A thin boot-beaten track leads me from the entryway into an adjacent patch of woodland. After the intensity of the sun on the trail I welcome the shade. I follow the invisible boundary wall of the former fort that the church replaced, finding my way under a canopy of elm, a tree long associated with feelings of melancholy and death and the preferred wood to be used to make coffins.

Inside the forest, the air is thick and I find it difficult to breathe. I walk slowly and cautiously, as though I am uncovering an ancient civilisation. The path ends behind a yurt and I move around its curved edge to find myself in the middle of a commune.

Begun in 1948, this is one branch of the Othona community, a group of Christians that provide a place for people of all ages and beliefs to come and spend time together on retreats, working the land, worshipping and studying. At the height of their programme of events, this particular site can hold up to a hundred followers. Yet now there is no one here, save for a lone, slightly sad-looking, middle-aged man sweeping leaves.

A small play area lies unused at its centre and I can't shake the ominous feeling of having stumbled into my own dystopian wasteland; the result of all I have been and all I have done.

Suddenly, I'm tired of observing landscapes when I should be immersing myself in them. I'm weary from sitting endlessly on the sidelines and allowing others to claim the power. I have lingered at the ends of the earth for too long. I look at the rusting bars of the children's climbing frame, and begin to formulate a plan. One where, this time, I will be in control.

EIGHT

Borderlines

My arms were aching. I'd been sat in the same position for what felt like hours learning how to tie knots and working out the best way to negotiate a rock-face while expending the least amount of energy. After my walk in Essex, I had signed up for a climbing course to literally show me the ropes. I was being taught not only how to correctly tie in, but also how to perform a rescue and, crucially, how to save myself if something went wrong.

Work had brought Jack temporarily closer to where I took my lessons and I met him afterwards. On a whim we decided to swim out to an island in the nearby river – not for any particular reason, but because we wanted to feel alive. His job was hard and 'grown-up'. He worked long hours and cared way more than his colleagues about targets and outcomes. He felt any failures in the workplace acutely – carrying them with him long after he clocked out. He told me he believed he wouldn't live beyond middle age – convinced that stress would be his ultimate end.

He reminded me of myself.

When the pub closed we snuck away to the tree-lined waterway, stripped to our underwear, packed our clothes into a dry bag and, guided by the light from the stars, swam out into the night.

Britain is a strange land to me. A collection of four countries so distinct from one another in so many ways. Growing up in Wales I felt it all too keenly – the way I spoke, no matter which side of the border I was on, was always a point of contention. England was typically at the centre, the place that governed the rest, the one whose flag, the St George's cross, a red rood on a white background, is also the international sign for protection. Its identity is all-encompassing and manages to seep in all directions, permeating into every distinct region in ways that are both overt and completely disguised.

Scotland perhaps has a much stronger self-image in comparison. Tough, forthright, determined, a land of fighters – it's what keeps leading to calls for another Referendum on whether or not it should break away from the rest of us.

Northern Ireland is problematic, a place defined by the phrase 'The Troubles' – its people torn between the land they are physically part of and their neighbour across the water. From my house in Wales it was easier to get to Dublin than it was London, a train ride to Holyhead and then over the sea to the Republic. And from Scotland, the island is closer still – you can be in Northern Ireland's capital of Belfast in just over two hours by regular ferry.

Wales itself has fought to take back some of its own ancient identity. The Welsh language is ubiquitous on all road signs; the clusters of consonants and circumflexes over vowels are so familiar to me that when I need to reduce speed I think of the word 'araf' before the English word 'slow', no matter where I am driving. In recent years, resurgence of spoken Welsh among younger people suggests we're keen to identify with our heritage. Acts of wanton disregard for Welsh people, such as the 1965 decision to flood a village near Bala to provide drinking water for the people of Liverpool, thereby displacing a whole community, undoubtedly planted a seed in people's minds that being ruled from London was unacceptable. Only decades later, in 1997, would the Senedd, or Welsh Parliament, be formed to allow for a devolved government to have more control over its own country.

The borderlines between us are fragile and fraught. Over time they have been negotiated, fought for and violently crossed. My own boundaries have been similarly tested, destroyed and are slowly being rebuilt. So, perhaps unsurprisingly, I find myself particularly drawn to the pilgrim paths that seek to cross the manmade boundaries we have constructed, unashamedly joining two things together that have often been at odds.

The St Cuthbert's Way is a prime example, linking Scotland with England, both enabling and forcing pilgrims to dally betwixt the two. Since 2012 the Roman Catholic Archbishop of St Andrews has been reviving a number of similar border-crossing pathways, all ending in the former ecclesiastical capital of Europe, under the banner 'The Way of St Andrews'. St Ninian's Way is one such trail that links the Scottish seaside town to Carlisle in northern England. St Wilfrid's Way goes even further, beginning in Hexham and crossing Hadrian's Wall to reunite pilgrims with Scotland.

The Welsh Cistercian Way, begun in 1998, is perhaps less bold. A month-long undertaking, it encircles the whole of Wales, though does entertain brief flirtations with its English neighbour's borderlines. But the St Winefride Pilgrim Trail sees people make a journey from England's Shrewsbury out to Holywell in Flintshire.

I simply cannot find a designated pilgrim path, however, linking Northern Ireland with the Republic – the St Brigid's Way comes closest, ending three kilometres south of the border, but never quite manages to cross.

Recently, the British Pilgrimage Trust launched a new route from Pembrokeshire over to County Wexford in

Ireland, seeking to join the two countries, and Britain with the EU, thus crossing water as well as land. But that in itself is not new. Many pilgrims once walked the Camino de Santiago from Britain, and in recent years new officially approved sections of Spain's pathway have begun this tradition again, with the most recent running from Reading in Berkshire (the seat of St James's veneration in medieval England) to Southampton, which was waymarked by yellow and blue scallop shells in 2022.

The Hampshire Pilgrim's Trail starts in Winchester Cathedral and crosses over the Channel to end in Normandy at Mont Saint-Michel – a tidal island once crossed on foot by medieval pilgrims during low tide, though it's now accessible permanently via a raised bridge. The belief in this trail's ability to bring visitors to the region means its re-establishment is even backed by Hampshire County Council.

In medieval times, people would covet a much longer pilgrim path and make a several-year-long journey to Jerusalem. Such was the importance of physical border crossings for pilgrims back then that during the height of the Crusades in 1123 – where Christians and Muslims fought for control over sacred religious sites – the Pope himself stepped in, urging people to either walk the Camino de Santiago if they were in Europe or, for the British and Irish, to undertake the Welsh St David's Way instead. That route begins at Fishguard, where boats would bring followers over from Ireland, and ends at the cathedral and shrine of the saint in Wales's smallest city on the Pembrokeshire coast.

The concept of a pilgrimage being something dangerous intrigued me. I loved the idea of a walking route having to be devised to guarantee a pilgrim safe passage. And that's how I found a one-day pilgrimage, in Cornwall – the St Michael's Way.

Re-established in 1994, it was based on an old shipping record that showed that when pilgrims were headed to Europe and making their way to the south coast to pick up a boat, many perished in the rough and treacherous waters around Land's End. To avoid this peril, an overland route was established, a coast-to-coast wander, from Lelant on the north shores of the Cornish peninsula, down to the south, ending with a visit to St Michael's Mount, the sister site of France's Mont Saint-Michel, also on a tidal island. The purpose of the route was to guarantee safety, and with everything that had been happening in my life, I reason that it is exactly what I need.

The sleeper train rocks from side to side once more but, this time, my phone is secured away in my bag and I am ensconced in bed, tucked under my duvet. As we race along the tracks I imagine the coast trundling by outside my darkened window. Unlike the Caledonian Sleeper between London and Scotland, which passes through English cities on the way to the high mountains, the Night Riviera exchanges the capital for a cliff-hugging ride above the Exe estuary, along the edges of the sea wall at Dawlish and Teignmouth, skirting the edges of the wind-scoured tors of Dartmoor National Park and over the River Tamar, before entering Cornwall and the cathedral city of Truro, passing through its saintly triumvirate of Austell, Erth and Ives, before ending at the historic shores of Penzance – Cornish for 'Holy Head'.

I wake just before St Erth – named after one of the Irish saints who bought Christianity to Cornwall – and alight to take a second early-morning train north to Lelant. The light is still intensifying from the dawn, and song thrushes sing a shrill and repetitive trill that causes me to sit up as though stirred by an alarm clock, as I wait dozily on the platform. The walk is just under 22 kilometres, and I decide I will do it in leisurely fashion, over a single day, before catching the next sleeper train back home.

The place where I begin already has religious connotations. Lelant is Cornish for 'Church Site of Anta', even though the name on the church here is dedicated to a man called St Uny. Seeing names and phrases etched in both English and Cornish makes me feel as though I've stepped

221

back into Wales. I love the duality and miss it living in England. Reading them makes me want to decode the words and learn the stories behind them.

Towers of giant viper's bugloss rise up from behind a garden wall and are already attracting bees and butterflies to their purple rosettes. I reach the church at the top of a small hill overlooking the Hayle estuary, where a signpost proudly sports the yellow and blue scallop shell sign, denoting that this is officially part of the Camino Inglés to Santiago.

The air is still, and the small granite church sits happily amid long grass and wild daisies, framed by trees and, on my visit, draped with strings of colourful bunting. Outside, there stands a simple wooden cross, not delicately carved in an intricate design, but constructed of two uncropped branches of a tree, tied together with twine. It feels less ostentatious than others I've seen before, and here, in this setting, somehow more befitting.

The saint this church is called after was another Irish missionary, but the other, older saint who came first is the one for whom the village is named. A Celtic woman, rather than a man. I wonder if she, Anta, would be put out to discover that her legacy has been lost over time to a male counterpart.

I leave the church and begin to follow the familiar signs for the Camino once more. It seems strange to be back on a pathway so linked to where my unexpected journey on pilgrim routes began years before. Here in my home country, under the sun of a cloudless sky, I am instantly transported elsewhere, across seas and borders in my mind.

On the island with Jack a few weeks before I took the train to Cornwall, we'd crossed a physical watery boundary in the darkness and found ourselves on an eyot surrounded by mist. It was as though we had escaped reality and stumbled upon an alternative and mysterious land, away from the problems and responsibilities of our humdrum lives.

We drank rum, and tested each other on places, on people and on experiences we'd had. We laughed so much that I cried with happiness. I wanted to live. Really live. I was content, in a state of bliss. The voice in my head that critiqued me without abatement had at last fallen silent.

The call of an owl was serenading us, and the leaves of a weeping willow provided an impenetrable curtain. Sat there, without meaning to, we were on the verge of crossing a borderline of our own.

On the path in Cornwall, I am looking for a holy well. It is marked on my map about a kilometre from St Uny's Church, but amid the huge thickets of gorse and bracken it is invisible to me. I leave the path, searching amid the leaves. I listen for the sound of water. But nature does not easily give away her secrets and I depart with dry hands.

The golden sands of Carbis Bay emerge ahead and the clear sea water moves in slow motion towards it. The path keeps me off the sand, and I obey it, heading inland past the suburban cluster of houses and up onto Worvas Hill.

I am destined for a lime-and-mortar monument, laid here in memory of John Knill – a local man who devised an annual ceremony that has taken place every St James's Day in July since 1801. It sees ten young dancing girls, the daughters of Cornish families, all dressed in white, watched over by two widows dressed in black, while a fiddler plays a song called 'The Furry Dance'.

I opt not to dance a jig, but I do stop to take a break and eat a large piece of flapjack. Since the end of my relationship with The Scientist I've begun to eat again. I am slowly accepting my flaws, allowing myself to taste the pleasures of life and not deny them. I have given myself permission to escape my own control, en route to a more positive path.

The mist was dissipating around the island in the river. The cry of a startled swan stopped Jack and me in our tracks as we both simultaneously realised that if we crossed this boundary there would be no going back. Jack pulled away and I felt shaken and confused. What were we doing?

Instantly we were both hit with regret. We hadn't fully committed to the path we shouldn't take, but we'd gone far enough along it. He started to talk about his family. I told him what had happened between us meant nothing, that nothing would change. I promised that I wouldn't say a word. It would be as if it had never happened.

We pulled on our clothes and sat in silence by the river-bank trying to fathom just what would happen next. The mist had cleared. The magic wall was gone. And we both had to face life on the other side.

Cornwall is a land of giants.

Ever since time began we humans have been storytell-ers. From drawing paintings on cave walls to illustrate a hunt, to whispering cautionary tales to children to keep them safe from real dangers such as deep bogs, expansive woodland and rough seas, we love to weave magic with our words and elucidate the unexplainable with legends. Arthurian myth is found all over Britain, as well as narra-tives of deceitful Selkies, and giants who sit on mountain tops. Usually, traces of these once common tales are hidden within place names, but in Cornwall there is no subtlety.

Here, even on the official government-sanctioned Ordnance Survey map, there are Piskies (Pixie) Caves and a Giant's Grave, and as I walk the St Michael's Way, on a National Trust sign I am advised that a huge granite boulder sits mysteriously by a stream after being discarded by two giants who were playing bowls.

I walk to the top of a Neolithic stone-wall enclosure, known as Trencrom Hill – temporarily leaving the waymarked trail. I stop and look south and catch my first glimpse of St Michael's Mount – where I will stand just hours later.

The rocks on this Iron Age hillfort form a cradle, a spoon and a chair for a giant called Trecobben. Folklore says that another giant, a lazy one called Cormoran, lived at Mount Bay, the place where my destination lies. He was jealous of the views the hillside giants were enjoying so ordered his wife Cormelian – said to be as tall as a cliff and strong as twenty horses – responsible for building their home, to construct the tidal island on which the church still sits.

Stories abound of Cormelian fetching huge rounds of granite from the moorland beneath where I am standing, collecting them in her apron, which was made of the leather from ten bulls. Meanwhile, Cormoran would lounge about, eating barrels of pilchards and napping for hours, filling the air with his thunderous snores.

Trecobben relished his vantage point and threw rocks as though playing a game with his coastal neighbour. In doing so, it is said, he created many of the knolls and ridges that make up the Penwith Moors. But one day he threw one aimed for Cormoran and mistakenly hit his wife instead. It is her grave that is marked on my map.

Up here there is another well in which water can be collected, to be dropped on St Michael's Mount when it is reached as an offer of penance for Trecobben's mistake. But I find no water available. I stop to eat again, a pasty filled with hearty chunks of cheese and onion. I gorge myself on it happily, feeling no regret or guilt. When I am done, I take to the path that leads me down into some trees and from there head to a ford over Red River.

The Cornish name for this place is Dowr Amal, Dowr meaning water, Amal meaning Boundary. I take off my shoes and socks and, eschewing the footbridge, cross it barefoot, feeling the cold water stinging my toes.

When we got back to the shore, and the island was lost to the black of night, Jack could look at me again. With tears in both our eyes, we agreed this had been a misstep, a near miss. He said he wanted to come clean to his wife, but we both knew if he did then our friendship would be over. Resolutely we promised ourselves we would not tell another soul. We vowed our friendship meant too much. We swore nothing would ever happen like this again. But, as we picked up the trail leading back towards the bright lights of town, he walked several steps ahead of me and never looked back. A physical gap was noticeably forming between us and I could only hope that time would allow us to forgive one another.

At Ludgvan Church a stone figure is carved above the entryway depicting a man in pilgrim robes clutching his wooden staff. Pilgrims have been coming here for centuries as it is yet another site of a holy well. It's thought to have been built in honour of a sixth-century Irish saint called Ludewon, but records proving his existence are scarce and dubious.

Even before Christianity took hold, it's believed pagans worshipped here at the water, giving thanks for the life-giving natural source that for them would have been rightfully sacred. Some also believed it to have a healing property that could cure blindness.

The building that stands here now is from the fourteenth century and is dedicated instead to the much better-known St Paul, one of Jesus' Apostles. And though the church is Christian, it too has been no stranger to magical beliefs: a vicar here once declared that anyone who was baptised using its special waters would never be hung by hemp rope. At a time when being hanged really wasn't that remote a possibility, this was a masterful way to get bums on pews.

When I visit, the well is long since gone, lost to time or perhaps destroyed during the Reformation. But this church also holds claim to being the last place to have had a service conducted in the native tongue, and was attended by the chemist Humphry Davy – famed for inventing the Davy Lamp, a specially designed portable oil-and-wick light source that, due to its use of internal mesh, would not explode if exposed to the methane gas often encountered by those working underground. As the granddaughter of a miner, I decide to light a candle of thanks before I leave.

As the church recedes into the distance, the light from my candle still glowing brightly in the dark, I recall reading in a guidebook that here among the pockets of sessile oak trees, the last wolf living in England was captured and killed at a place called Rospeith. Sharing my love of legends and wildlife, I know that if he had been here, Jack would have immediately suggested we go on a fruitless mission to find and locate it, camping within the trees and howling to the moon.

I leave my feral thoughts behind temporarily as I find myself on the edge of Tremenheere Sculpture Gardens, a place where modern art blooms from behind exotic flowers, and people come to drink coffee and buy sub-tropical species hoping they will survive in their homes.

Once the property of the monks of St Michael's, this plot was sold in 1295 to a local tenant farmer called Michael De Tremenheere. Thanks to its unique microclimate, which allows the exotic trees and flowers to thrive, it was formerly a vineyard for the monks. Now it's something of a tourist attraction and home to a very popular café.

I wander past the people sitting enjoying their food and the sunshine. It feels strange to be in the company of so many others when minutes earlier my mind has been away with the wolves.

Fields of maize remind me that this area is still very much the domain of farmers, and a helicopter taking off over towering hedges of bracken, destined for the Scilly Isles, suggests the tourist side of Cornwall is soon going to be unavoidable.

I add on the optional leg of an extended path to reach a parish that holds the remains of one of the oldest mines in the region as well as the church at Gulval, where Jesus himself was said to have visited with his father Joseph when he was just a lowly carpenter (though the dates make this impossible). On my arrival, the building is shut tight and all

I can do is admire the grave of a John Thomas, emblazoned with a pirate's skull and crossbones. In classic Cornish folklore fashion he is said to have been a smuggler from Marazion whose church refused to take his body, though no records back up this account.

I leave my diversion to rejoin the main path for the final leg of the pilgrimage to St Michael's Mount. I look to the side of the now asphalt promenade and see the invasive species of Mexican fleabane poking out from between the cracks. I spot a bloom of the edible flowers of *Brassica nigra* and pull off the leaves, the bitter flare of mustard exploding in my mouth.

The tide is rushing in when I reach the causeway that will lead me to St Michael's, so I approach a National Trust volunteer and ask if I can take his boat instead. But the vessel is fully booked and the tide will not retreat before I have to catch my train home.

I sit on the sand and lament a little, about how I won't be able to see the great rock that once would have been part of the mainland, covered by trees; won't get to gaze inside the Giant's Well into which Cormoran, after years of terrorising local farmers, fell and died. I am sad to think I will miss out on spotting the heart-shaped stone, said to have belonged to the giant, that's embedded in its foundations. And the church of St Michael, where an archangel is said to have appeared to a fisherman, and where one of unlucky-in-love St Dwynwen's sisters – St Keyne, a nomadic hermitess – went to meet her nephew St Cadoc of Glamorgan in the sixth century, who persuaded her to return home to Wales.

I resign myself to disappointment and instead decide to wade out to Chapel Rock, much nearer the beach, to mark the end of this journey. Back at the height of pilgrimage, a shrine to St Mary is believed to have stood here. As I near it, I recognise it instead as being from the story of the giants. This stone is one that Cormelian is said to have collected while her lazy husband slept. She decided she wouldn't climb uphill to get a piece of granite for him any more, and instead opted to pick up a lump of greenstone that lay in the woods nearby. As she walked past him, carrying it, he was awoken by a seagull, who sat on his nose and made him sneeze. When he saw what she was doing, he gave her a kick for her insolence, causing her apron strings to snap and the rock within its folds to fall into the sand, where it still lies now.

I stand on the top of its slippery surface and feel a kinship with Cormelian.

The time has come to go home, however, and I take out my phone to check the train times. Jack and I have managed to get back on an even keel after our indiscretion. We've walked again, laughed again, but something has definitely shifted. It is as though we are both having to be extra guarded around each other, worried that neither one of us knows where this friendship could go next.

I've messaged him several times on my Cornish walk but heard nothing, so decide to give him a call.

When he answers he tells me, very calmly, that I need to stop contacting him.

Shocked, I ask what has changed.

'I've told her,' he says. 'And we can no longer be friends.'

I turn off my phone and watch the screen go black. Then I run down to the sea and without even removing my jacket I plunge under the surface, seeking solace beneath the waves.

Temporarily removed from the world above, I never want to come back.

NINE

Wander Woman

The critical voice in my head had returned, an omni-present nagging doubt that I am ever good enough or even capable of doing the right thing. Meanwhile my therapist had abandoned me, moving away to start a new life elsewhere.

I tried to find a new counsellor from her recommendations. One made an appointment with me then cancelled, then another did the same. Finally, an older lady said she would meet me for an introductory session, free of charge, to see if she felt she could help.

Her house was modern on the outside, but inside the couches were cracked red leather and the doilies felt too fussy and at odds with the exterior. I had an hour. And so used it to tell her the situation I had recently found myself in, again. I announced dramatically that I was a home-wrecker. I had given up a steady relationship – troubled though it was – and immediately had fallen into this new, tawdry role. Women my age were getting married or having children, and here I was destroying their happiness. It was as if I'd missed a signpost for the path I should have taken, even though I knew I didn't want to take it.

I told her about Jack, about the night we nearly went too far. She looked at me concerned.

'This isn't your fault,' she said without flinching. There was no apparent judgement, no look of disgust. Her hair was pinned up tight in curls that reminded me of the perm my granny used to get. 'Two of you were there. Why should any fault be yours alone?'

'Because I knew he had a family. I should never have allowed us to even get into the situation where something could have happened.'

'Why?'

'Because ... because I should always be the one to make things better.'

She let the phrase hang in her pink living room, while I felt around in a tissue box covered with a knitted shroud.

I blew my nose, the noise breaking the silence.

'I know what you feel,' she finally said. 'In your world everyone abandons you. They let you down. Your parents abandoned you by giving you an ultimatum that you felt had only one outcome: that you had to leave. Then your mother abandoned you, not by choice, but still she left you with responsibilities to look after everyone. Your friends abandoned you because you changed; then you pushed them away, and they didn't fight back. And the relationships you've sought since, you've chosen with the expectation that they will eventually abandon you too. That has become your comfortable place. As uncomfortable as it may make you feel.'

From her nearby kitchen I could smell something cooking in the oven. Its homely scent of gravy tugged at memories from the tapestry of my past.

'But I'm afraid I cannot help you,' she said.

She explained how she was winding down her clients for retirement. And my situation was too complex to 'fix' in the time she had left.

When it comes to religion, or Christianity at least, women have a very definite role – usually chaste and revered, like the Virgin Mary, or subjected to a downtrodden life and a role of subjugation. All the apostles were men and most saints (as well as being wealthy) are male too, outnumbering women at least three to one. So far I had not found many famous pilgrim paths that walkers can take to follow in the footsteps of female holy figures.

There are some. In Cumbria, the St Bega's Way runs for 65 kilometres between the priory at St Bees on the coast, to St Bega's church in Bassenthwaite. Rumoured to be an Irish princess in the ninth century, St Bega was betrothed to a Viking prince. But not wanting to give up her virginity, she fled overseas to England and set up a hermit cell in a cave on the coast so that she could live a life of piety and sexual abstinence. She took with her a bracelet that was thought to have been given to her by a heavenly being. However, fearing the invasion of pirates who could steal 'the most precious treasure with which heaven can endow her sex' – that is, her virginity – she then made her way from the coast and across the fells to settle at Bassenthwaite Lake, where she lived out her days untouched by any man. Today the church that stands in her name celebrates her as a virgin saint, though as an interesting aside, the plaque that stands next to it shouts more loudly about the Norman building's association with Lord Alfred Tennyson, who was inspired to write a poem there.

Up in Scotland the little-known St Margaret's Way follows waterways and former railway lines from Edinburgh, for 100 kilometres. It passes over the Forth Road Bridge (where Margaret established a ferry to enable pilgrims to cross the water on their journey) to follow the coast alongside the island of Inchcolm – once known as the 'Iona of the East' – where ruins of a twelfth-century abbey (shattered by the English in the Reformation) can be found, until finally it ends in St Andrews. The eponymous eleventh-century saint of this trail was known for her 'fidelity' to the Roman Catholic Church – and for being 'pure' and a married woman.

Finally, Wales has its own female-led pathway, once more a virgin, Winefride of Holywell – the one whose head was cut off when she refused the advances of her suitor and who was gifted new life by St Bueno for her chastity.

In religion, it seems women are valued more for their virginity and purity than for any quantifiable deeds. In that respect I knew, in the eyes of God, I had most definitely failed. Had I been a character in the Bible I would have certainly been predisposed to come to a gruesome and grisly end.

I could see clearly down the path I now seemed to be treading and didn't want to walk it any more.

I needed a strong woman to follow.

That's when I found Hilda.

Born amid the throes of civil wars, following the collapse of the Roman Empire in Britain, this seventh-century saint lost her father as a young child and went to live with her great uncle – a king – in what was then Northumbria. She was exposed to religion at the age of thirteen when he had his entire family baptised. Little is known about her life between then and when she became a nun at thirty-three, but I like to think that is because she took those years to live a little. At the time Hilda took her vows, the two main religions were Roman and Celtic Christianity. Though baptised in the former, she seemed to embrace the latter and was summoned by Aidan of Lindisfarne to come and lead a monastery as abbess in Whitby.

What is known about her charge, called Streanæshalch, is that, unlike others, it was a co-ed abbey, where nuns and monks lived together. Hilda famously declared, despite her privileged roots, that 'no one was rich, none poor, for they had all things common'.

During her time there she became celebrated for her ability to bring out the best in others. Under her tutelage five monks went on to become bishops, and one – Cædmon – became the first named English poet. It was said that Hilda had inspired him to find his voice.

The final fact I read about Hilda (sometimes referred to as Hild, meaning battle) was that she was said to have purged the land of all snakes, which she turned to stone. Those snakes are always shown in effigies and icons of her, though a closer inspection reveals them to be ammonites – the extinct carnivorous shelled cephalopods (molluscs) that died out about 66 million years ago and whose closest living relatives today are squids and cuttlefish. Now, as would have been possible back then, a walk along this Yorkshire coastline (often marketed by the tourist board as the 'Dinosaur Coast') reveals hundreds of examples of these ancient creatures, and there are tales of local artisans who would collect them from the beach and carve on them snakes' heads to sell to pilgrims in time gone by. She even gave one genus of these ancient creatures their scientific name: *Hildoceras*.

I loved the way that in this legend, natural history had merged seamlessly with religious belief. And the thought of following in the footsteps of a woman determined to rid our lives of sneaky and deceitful serpents seemed pretty apt.

So I made my way resolutely to a village called Hinderwell in the North York Moors National Park, hoping that her famous guiding light would show me the way forward.

The Victorian glass of the eighteenth-century church window allows spindles of colourful light to pass through it, causing a sprinkle of rainbow to fall on the stone floor at my feet. Above, a star hangs from the wooden rafters, while crosses made of a single piece of folded reed are left on the pews from a service held before I arrived.

This is St Hilda's Church, but without even knowing its name I could have guessed that a powerful woman was at the heart of the building. Beneath the organ a mosaic shows a lady, dressed as a nun, clasping a building in one hand, while in the other she holds a pilgrim's staff topped with the swirl of an ammonite. On one side of her, the waves have parted to allow her safe passage, while over her shoulder a den of snakes hurries away, banished. Even the windows are dedicated to her legacy, with one depicting her image surrounded by other praying women, with a crown and her staff beneath her feet.

In 2015 the Dean of Whitby decided he wanted to create a pathway to celebrate this female saint, and no doubt encourage people to explore his parish. It's called the St Hilda's Way and in my hand I clutch the only guide to it that currently exists, written by a retired vicar and her husband who now live in Flamborough, further to the south of the abbey that marks the end of the 70-kilometre trail.

On the book's instruction, I head outside the church and walk around to the back of the building to find the holy well – St Hilda's Well – thought to have inspired the name of the village in which it sits (Hinderwell). Covered with a stone slab to form a roof, it's a small pocket of water, edged by verdant spleenwort, and flows rather than stands still. Said to have emerged here when Hilda herself was on a pilgrimage and in need of water, it has been used for baptisms for many years.

One thing I hadn't realised was that when you are baptised, the water should always be moving. It is believed that the flow of the liquid is what physically takes away your sins and carries them far away.

Before I set off for Yorkshire, I'd helped my dad clear out some boxes he'd found in the attic. In them, I found a certificate of baptism for myself, physical proof of my mum christening me 'just in case'. It confirmed that it had been completed using water from the River Jordan, where Jesus himself is said to have been baptised.

I plunge my hands into the water at St Hilda's Well, following the book's instructions as though my future depends on it. I feel the cold begin to sting my fingertips but resolve to leave them there while my mind wanders to Jordan, and the river whose water I felt on my temples soon after leaving the womb.

St Hilda is known for her ability to handle delicate issues with grace and wisdom. She famously sat at the table when the Synod of Whitby was making the decision whether to celebrate Easter using the Roman system or the Celtic one. They both used a lunar cycle based on the first Sunday after the Full Moon, but calculated this differently, which caused a number of issues – mainly that people began to question Christianity altogether. Hilda believed in the Celtic way, having trained under Aidan of Lindisfarne, but the vote saw the Roman way proving the winner, based on something a man, St Peter, had said. As the then king believed Peter held the keys to the gates of heaven, he felt it was probably worth keeping him on-side. When the vote didn't go Hilda's way, she accepted it without question and taught it to her followers, encouraging them to embrace the new way.

As I walk across a patch of woodland marked on the map as The Dales, crossing over a footbridge edged by hazel trees – once known as the 'tree of knowledge' – I contemplate my own saintly namesake. Called a 'deacon' by Paul, St Phoebe was one of the earliest saints, as long ago as the first century, and the only one to have been labelled with this ministerial title in the Bible. She was even bestowed with her own saint's day of celebration. Little known today, her importance has been questioned and dismissed endlessly by scholars unconvinced that a woman could reach those lofty heights back then. I made a note to remember and celebrate her on 3 September.

I make my way across Borrowby Moor, through a field full of harebells. Related to the bluebell, these purple flowering wild plants are often associated with women, sometimes called lady's or fairy's thimbles, or witches' bells (as they are said to produce a milk that witches use to turn themselves into hares and escape capture). The female dichotomy continues even in the plant world: you can either be a fairy or a witch.

I move through another cluster of woodland, passing felled trunks covered in polypore fungi and ash trees – a genus of tree the Norse believe gave birth to the very first man – which in this forest are being strangled by endless vines of ivy.

At Scaling Reservoir I trace the manmade dam alongside a road, the roar of car engines humming in my ears, disorientating me amid a landscape that previously felt so far removed from the human world.

The next section of the route follows contours up and over High Moor to reach Beacon Hill – the loftiest point on the entire trail. The moors feel desolate, and I tread under the gun-metal grey sky feeling cold.

At the top of an incline, a metal beacon signifies that I have reached the highest point and I look over the moorland that spreads out from beneath my feet. It is sometimes yellow, sometimes splashed with the off-purple of heather that has recently perished, and often edged by thick hedgerows defining boundaries between the farmland.

I descend into the village of Danby, where I've arranged to stay. It isn't yet dark when I reach it and so I decide to keep walking to the next church. Situated a couple of kilometres from the small centre, I trace single-track lanes and smell wild garlic on the wind.

When I reach the 500-year-old building, I note how its graveyard pleasingly follows the undulations of the land on which it sits. Inside, a stained-glass window depicts the meeting at the Synod of Whitby where Hilda sat between two opposing sides.

After Jack ended our friendship, I realised two things. The first was that it is possible for me to experience happiness with another person. Jack had given me a glimpse of what it could be like when I spent time with someone who shared my passions. The second was that I needed to become more open-minded about my friendships with women. Having only male close friends was a comfort zone but one in which I was no longer comfortable.

I was invited to a female friend's book launch, a successful woman with an illustrious music career who I've admired for many years. She was performing readings for a large crowd, interspersing song and anecdotes. To the whole room she appeared the epitome of success. Yet a question caught her off-guard. What does she think is the key to happiness?

She thought about it for a while and then said simply: 'To be loved.'

Leaving Danby the next morning I curse the trail for taking me along a single-track road, complete with speeding cars that seem to appear in an instant.

At last, the pale blue ammonite symbols that mark the trail lead me into the town of Lealholm, where the route runs parallel to both the River Esk and the train to Middlesbrough and Whitby, via Nunthorpe.

Here, the St Hilda's Way makes a clear transition, from moor to riverside. Where everything before seemed bleak and endless, it is now winding and full of promise.

At Glaisdale Station there is a scheduled monument in the form of a packhorse bridge built over the river in 1619. It's said to have been constructed by Tom Ferris, a once lowly boy who was rejected by his lover's father for being too poor. He resolutely declared he would head to the coast to seek his fortune on the oceans. When he went to say goodbye to his beloved, the river was too wide for him to cross, and so he left without a kiss. When he returned years later, having made his fortune, he built a bridge so that the water would never stop two lovers meeting again.

I continue through woodland, now following the leaping salmon waymarkers for the Esk Valley Walk. The water is virtually silent as I pick my way along the dirt path surrounded by the tooth-edged lobes of sycamore leaves. Every so often, I spy the remnant of a bushcraft-style lean-to den sitting beneath sturdy tree trunks. As I climb higher, beneath the shining white bark of silver birch, curved stones mark the route, worn down into grooves that resemble smiles from years of footfall. Something about this process, treading where so many boots have trodden before, makes my stirring mind settle.

By the time I reach the water at Egton Bridge, its babbling notes are soothing. I decide to abandon the safety of a footbridge and instead leap over the river on stepping stones, telling myself that with each jump I am temporarily flying.

The first church here is named after one of Hilda's students – St Hedda – and contains the remains of Nicholas Postgate, an eighty-year-old who in the seventeenth century practised mass and baptism up on the moors, despite these being banned. He was betrayed, and hung, drawn and quartered for his actions. Despite the macabre death associated with the place, the church is an open and airy building, sporting a rounded dome roof that is full of light. Outside, the tiny purple flowers of butterfly bushes splash any dreariness with colour. I notice a small tortoiseshell fluttering between the conical blooms and watch as it reveals its two very different sides – dull, dark brown wings underneath, which open to reveal a dazzling topcoat of orange, purple, black and white. He is not one thing; he is many. He has been a caterpillar and a cocoon already. He had to change and transform in order to survive.

The trail passes St Hilda's Church at Egton, which has no vicar so stays locked. I look up to see the backside of the stained-glass window of Hilda. From the outside it appears merely as a cluster of blues, purples and blacks, but despite my skewed perspective I can see her ammonite-topped staff so know I am on the right track.

I take the train back to Danby, to find the owner of the apartment I am staying in has left me a book about all the saints. In it I find the chapter on Hilda, which recounts her prayer. I read her words:

Take me often from the tumult of things
into Thy presence.
There show me what I am

My mum was a strong woman who, like me, counted more men among her friends than women. She rarely wore make-up and so I never learned how to apply it myself. She was a walking set of contradictions. She was proudly feminist and fought for women's rights, but then said she wished feminists would look pretty rather than manly. When I was growing up she said that women posing naked in photographs was derogatory, but then raved about a picture of the model Sophie Dahl in which she proudly lay prone on a velvet blanket looking – in my mum's words – 'strong and powerful'. She made jokes about how she ruled the roost at home, but when I asked if I could keep living there, she told me it was my dad's decision.

When my life became complicated, I directed more of my anger at her than my dad. But in death she seemed to acquire a kind of sainthood for me, whereby I no longer felt I could criticise her at all. I am sure my dad found that difficult.

At one time I had resolved not to be like her, yet I think subconsciously I hoped I would be. I always tried to please her and still try to now, even though she will never be around to utter the words I long to hear: 'I'm proud of you, you are enough.'

I am starting to realise her relationship with me – and then the sudden absence of it – affected me more than I ever have allowed myself to acknowledge. Her contradictions have played out in me. Her hates have made me hate myself. Her judgements made me my own worst critic.

But she also told me, before she died, that I was her dancing star. I hope I can be that for myself.

My final day on the trail sees me edging away from the river towards the coast. Names on the map nod to more ecclesiastical links. I pass Priory Farm and St Oswald's Close. Then another church bearing Hilda's name, in

Sneaton, before I finally lay my eyes on my journey's end at Whitby. There on a hill above the town are the ghostly arches of Hilda's once grand abbey, towering above the waves.

I take the trail still known as Monk's Walk, where it's assumed pilgrims have trodden for centuries en route to Whitby. I wonder how many women like me were among the lost souls looking for answers.

Reaching the edge of town I pass Sneaton Castle – a wedding venue, but also home to St Hilda's Priory where the Order of the Holy Paraclete, a women-only religious community, live. Called 'sisters', they take vows of poverty, celibacy and obedience in what is known in religious circles as a 'calling'. They also come here to be cared for in old age and illness. They believe that everyone has a calling. I think that mine, if I have one, might be to simply wander, to never settle.

In Whitby itself a town trail can be followed, taking in several religious buildings. I decide to go first to St Hilda's Anglican Church. It is located just behind a junction on the main road that takes drivers to the waterfront, and from the outside appears imposing. Above the front door a stone carving of Hilda stands, clutching a model of the abbey in her hands.

Inside, it is just as grand, with a huge colourful angel-adorned altar and a giant stained-glass window immortalising the saint. I wonder if she would have wanted something so ostentatious in her name. As I leave, I nearly knock over a statue of her by the door. Painted in full colour, her robes are blue, though chipped and showing white plaster specks, and underneath her yellowed gown is fading in the light. She is wearing an expression that looks a little bored and I wonder how many sides to this woman there really were.

I stood in front of the photographer shaking slightly.

'It's okay,' she reassured me, 'you are in complete control.'

I was wearing high heels that were too big for my feet.

She moved me into position, raising my arm above my head to rest next to a mirror.

'It's time,' she advised, and I dropped the silk robe I was wearing and stood there naked in nothing but a pair of shoes.

After the way things ended with Jack, I'd started to get nervous about how things had ended with The Scientist. He had so many compromising photos of me and could, at any time, make them public.

Then one day, sick of feeling like a victim, I went to a boudoir photographer to get her to take pictures of me in her studio.

When I arrived, all the other women were there to get photographs taken for their partners, often as a wedding or anniversary gift. But I went to get these pictures taken just for me. So that I could see myself the way I wanted to, not through the gaze of another man. I chose my poses before I even went into the room, and let a woman do my hair and make-up. I was nervous but excited.

The whole process of getting the pictures done took barely half an hour, but by the time I'd finished I felt I'd regained a huge amount of control over my own body. I alone had chosen to capture this. I would get the images to keep and I would decide what to do with them, even if I did nothing at all.

It was one of the most powerful decisions I made. And on my way home I celebrated by eating all the foods I'd been craving, but for so long had not allowed myself to enjoy.

On my final approach to the abbey I spot a blossom of chicory, a violet-coloured edible plant whose flower looks to me like a cluster of sunrays. It is known to gardeners for its strong fertility and in European folklore is said to be the plant that can unlock a magic door into unseen worlds, and even help those who carry it forget past loves.

The church of St Mary's, positioned between the ruined abbey and the town, is thought to be close to the site of the original monastery, if not on it. Here Cædmon's Cross, named for the poet whose talent Hilda nurtured, stands proud. Represented is Hilda atop her snakes; at her feet are the five bishops she trained. It is a final powerful image: a woman fighting demons, teaching others and taking her own path above men, wherever it may lead her.

History states that Hilda was often sought by leaders, including kings and queens, for her wisdom and guidance. She continued to work right up until she died, spending the last six years of her life ill but dedicated. I can only hope to be as stoical.

Hilda's legacy has become more prominent in the last few years, and in 2020 a second, coastal St Hilda's Way was opened by Hartlepool Borough Council. I read that Hilda always thought she would leave Britain for France, to be united with her sister in a convent there, but life pulled her in a different direction. Had it not, our history would be different – and not just for the religious. Her abbey inspired artists, writers and poets, gave a leg up to people in poverty, and allowed women everywhere to see the power of a female figure at the helm.

I stop beneath the stone walls of Whitby Abbey to wander amid the gothic arches, which are all that remain of this eleventh-century structure. It was built after Hilda's was destroyed by Danes in successive raids between 867 and 870, remaining derelict for more than two hundred years before Reinfrid, a soldier of William the Conqueror, founded a new monastery here. I mourn a little as I read that after Hilda died her community became a monastery for Benedictine monks, where women were no longer allowed.

I look up to see a pair of kittiwakes flying high above the building, on their way out to sea. There is one final legend here, which states that when sea birds fly over the abbey at Whitby they dip their wings in honour of St Hilda.

Her settlement may not have lasted, but following her trail has left a mark on me. It reminds me that changing direction or pausing on a path is not failure. Stopping can be a sign of strength rather than weakness. Change is inevitable.

In the book about the saints left in my Airbnb, the final page on St Hilda ends with a prayer:

May the ending of my pilgrimage be the joyful beginning of the rest of my life.

I am not religious, but I will say amen to that.

TEN

Evensong

I am standing on top of a burial mound high above the English Channel. The grass at my feet has been worn away by centuries of pilgrims passing through and is now a bald patch on what looks like an ageing, yellowed scalp. From here I can see forests and fields stretching out infinitely ahead. Paths criss-cross below me, offering endless possibilities. But the choice of which route I take has already been made. I am not alone but with a group of fifteen people all on a single day's pilgrimage.

Beside me a woman with blonde curly hair gazes out into the distance, lost temporarily in thought. Next to her a man clutches a wooden staff – he has walked on pilgrim trails before – and shares her pensive gaze. They do not know each other, but they do share this common ground.

The small hill on which I stand is one of four on the top of Bow Hill, in West Sussex, named the Devil's Humps. On the next small summit three people are standing tall, while the remaining congregation either sit or lie down on the grass. One places their forehead to the earth as though trying to burrow beneath it, or at least commune with whatever exists beneath its banks.

Not a single word is uttered between us. This is a silent pilgrimage.

Once again, I learned of this new concept from the British Pilgrimage Trust. It feels strange to be back on one of their guided trips, walking another section of The Old Way. This one, though, feels markedly different. Or maybe I do.

In the months since walking with St Hilda I had, little by little, begun to try to accept who I was, what I had done, and what I will do going forwards. When the negative voice inside my head began to condemn me, instead of trying to escape it, I acknowledged it, I accepted it, and I let it sit with me rather than push it away.

I still didn't have a new therapist. So, instead of talking, I started to write.

When I was in primary school, because both my parents worked full-time I had to stay on at the end of the official day with a child-minder. I remember I was asked to join a creative writing club and so I did. My friends seemed to think I was crazy, choosing to do written work for fun, but I loved it. There was something about wielding a pen that made me feel I could do anything. Amid the lines on the page I could journey wherever I chose, I could run riot and be messy, and no one was able to stop me.

Later, in another school, a teacher told me I held my pen wrong. She tried to force me to hold it 'like everyone else'. I hated her for it. My writing became alien to me; scratchy, small and illegible. When she was reassigned to another class I began to write in my own way again, and with it returned my enjoyment of the process.

In my final year at that school, we were set a challenge to write a story with an overt theme. I chose circles and described a room with a big round door, round windows and circular tables. The teacher was so impressed she sent a note to my parents telling them she saw a flair in me. When I got home I continued to work on the story, imagining a world where there were no straight edges.

That same teacher told us we had to start keeping diaries that would be 'marked for completion, not read'. I trusted her, though soon realised she did read them in detail and would use my own words against me in class. So my entries became sparse and impersonal.

In high school a teacher stopped me as I was leaving English class and told me she thought I had a gift with words. I batted her compliments away as misguided – I wasn't getting the highest grades on tests so she must be wrong.

I did always have a tendency to write myself out of problems that arose – from the innocuous, such as writing a letter to my mum explaining how hurt I was when she bought herself the pair of paisley Dr Martens boots that I had wanted, to penning secret poems during tumultuous relationships.

Once I got into my first controlling relationship I stopped the practice. The risk of discovery was too great, the consequences too severe. I think that's what drew me to a career where I could write about the world instead.

The silent pilgrimage has been scheduled to begin in the run-up to Christmas, offering people the opportunity to reflect on their lives away from the frenetic pace of life at this time of year.

Since Mum died, I'd struggled with Christmas as well as Easter. It's difficult to force yourself to be happy when there's an empty seat at the table and you can't really talk about it for fear of upsetting others. Christmas became a time to push through and survive, rather than embrace and enjoy. I would always feel relief after Boxing Day as things gradually returned to 'normal'.

Since Mum's death I'd previously always busied myself away from the festivities by heading abroad on assignment and immersing myself in countries where Christmas is not celebrated. More recently, though, I set myself challenges that purposely took place over the festive season, so that I could do something good to help others in difficult circumstances. I slept on the top of the three highest peaks in Britain, alone, to raise money for charity. I dressed up as Wonder Woman to walk the width of England, following Hadrian's Wall, sleeping in a bivvy bag, and battling frost and rain. It felt good to do something that benefited others, even though it meant enforcing solitude on myself at a traditional time of togetherness.

In the interim I'd become good friends with an adventurer called Dwayne after we met at a Duke of Edinburgh event in London. We were giving out awards to young people and both felt like imposters. We didn't know it when we first met but we would end up spending the entire month of December together – ending my run of lonely Christmases.

Originally from Jamaica, he grew up in London and escaped gang crime. On the surface we had nothing in common, yet the more we talked the more we realised we were actually very similar. We connected instantly and decided to work together, setting up a charity to try to make a difference to the lives of underprivileged young people who had found themselves on destructive life paths. Using 'adventures' as our most powerful tool, we wanted to show them that other opportunities were available.

It wasn't plain sailing. At a meeting in London with people who boasted about their legacy of helping to enable exploration, I was told that there were 'plenty of younger, prettier, sexier girls than you' who would get their support instead. Once more, I was keenly aware of being judged as a woman, stripped down and defined by my age and how I looked, rather than by my actions and what I was doing as a human being.

This time, though, I didn't let it stop me. I had a team-mate in Dwayne who believed in me too. So we literally walked our own path, fundraising for our first group of young people's trip – to Antarctica – by walking over forty days and nights (including Christmas Day) the length of mainland Britain, pulling all our kit in wheeled sleds and camping in laybys, between hedges and in farmers' fields under pylons, from the true north of the mainland, to the true south. I learned a lot from that trip, and even now – whenever the negative voices start becoming too loud – try to internalise its lessons: that people on the whole are wonderful and kind, that everyone is looking for a connection, that anything is possible.

I had met someone new as well. I'd signed up for another, separate charity adventure, this time for the local

Air Ambulance, with an old friend I'd reconnected with called John, who worked for them as a doctor. Together we kayaked and camped wild over ten nights, paddling mainly in the dark, starting on the autumn equinox, on a network of waterways spanning nearly 500 kilometres that encircled the medical team's patch. Along the way, critical care paramedics for the service came to see us and bring us hot food and drinks. One of them, I soon learned, was single.

He came to see us three times during the challenge, once to join us for a paddle near Oxford, bringing a borrowed inflatable kayak. John, seemingly acting as matchmaker, insisted he temporarily take the seat behind me in our kayak so that we could 'talk'. Having undertaken several expeditions himself as a medic, when on sabbatical from working on the helicopter and ambulances in London, he teased me about not looking after my feet, which were practically held together with blister plasters and duct tape.

We shared our love of walking, climbing and being outside. I had invented a jousting game using my paddle to scoop up crab-apples bobbing in the Thames and flip them over my shoulder – he successfully caught every single one. I was impressed. We laughed endlessly, and I loved the way his chuckle was loud and enormous and completely unguarded. A few weeks later we went out for a drink, just the two of us.

I wasn't even sure if it was a date when I headed to the pub to meet him, though I felt a pleasant tingling in my stomach that had been absent for so long. I did not set expectations. At first I was all bravado. We both said how much we loved our lives, commented on friends who had married and had kids and agreed that wasn't for us. We laughed a lot, talked a lot. He asked to see me again immediately.

Over the weeks, I tried things I thought from previous relationships were expected of me – but he stopped me, telling me I didn't need to. And when I did, a remarkable thing happened. He stayed. He seemed to love me for it. He was respectful. He gave me space. This felt healthy. Our dates involved wild swimming, night walks and climbing. I didn't have to pretend I liked something I didn't. I felt free to be me.

In the forest that sits just outside Bristol he came to see me and Dwayne on our walk across Britain just before Christmas and spent the night with me in my tent. He left me a gift. I began to allow myself to think this might be real.

When I arrive to start the silent pilgrimage, at a small church in Stoughton, rural West Sussex, it is just me and the group leader – Abigail. The air is so cold on this

December morning that when I exhale and plumes of condensation emerge from my nose, it looks as though I am breathing fire.

Abigail explains that she'd come up with the idea to get people to walk a single day's section of The Old Way in silence, as she believes time spent without talking outside can be pleasant at worst and healing at best.

Before we start properly, and while I can still chat to my fellow pilgrims, I engage several in conversation – eager to hear their reasons for participating. Kathryn is there to try and refocus her thoughts on what Christmas is really all about; José, originally from Mexico, is walking the route for his wife who can't make it due to childcare and has sent him under strict instruction to report back on the experience; a man called Lincoln has brought his friend from the Isle of Wight so they can try and reconnect. Then there is Sally, an older lady, who describes herself as gay and a regular churchgoer. She wants to try and square her own experience with the beliefs of a hostile Church that says her lifestyle is a sin. Others include a person recently diagnosed with a serious health condition, a spiritual Wiccan and a self-confessed pilgrimage addict who walked the Camino many years ago and has since been attracted to anything 'pilgrim' related.

Abigail tells us to search around on the ground to find an object, which she calls 'an intention', which will be a physical representation of something we will be thinking about, be it a person or situation, while we walk.

I begin my hunt at the corner of the graveyard, finally settling on the husk of a triangular beech nut. The nut itself provides a source of food and nourishment, though tastes slightly bitter. But the husk that surrounds it is spiky. It is well protected, invincible even, yet the bark of the tree from which it came scars easily, prone to lovers' graffiti, their carved initials remaining there even as the tree grows older and tries to heal. This handiwork will become fainter, but will never truly disappear.

The vicar, the Reverend Lindsey Yates, arrives by car, and comes to say hello to me. She is quite young, her dark hair pulled back into a ponytail, and she wears thick-rimmed glasses. She tells me that having a pilgrimage start here is a blessing. I ask her how she feels, as a religious woman, about most people on this walk not being Christians. She says it doesn't matter. What matters is that they are here at all.

Anxious chatter continues in the graveyard – as though everyone is trying to get their last words out before they can no longer speak. Then the reverend summons us inside, and as we walk into the church Abigail presents us all with a candle, telling us that later we will stop in another to eat our lunch away from the elements and will need the light.

She reads to us the famous poem 'Leisure', by W. H. Davies, which contains the famous lines:

> *What is this life if, full of care,*
> *We have no time to stand and stare*

As we leave the building we emerge into the world in complete silence.

Just days after my mum died in August 2001, the world materially changed through an event that sent shock waves around the globe. In the weeks that followed 9/11, a time when I was desperately trying to readjust to life after Mum, the world was suddenly plunged into mourning too. When I tried to tell anyone, back then, that I was struggling with my own devastating tragedy, it was always against this very visceral backdrop – one in which thousands of people were going through something arguably a lot worse.

Sometimes I could see it written on people's faces if I tried to talk to them – they would say something like: 'Well at least you knew she was ill and had time to say goodbye – not like those in the Twin Towers ...'

When I was in therapy I was told that comparing my problems with the suffering of others around the world was unhelpful. Known as 'comparative suffering' it means that because you assess your own situation against other tragedies, you prevent yourself from feeling entirely natural reactions, resulting in a kind of mental blockage that can be extremely detrimental. This same pattern is also true of celebrating successes, something I have also been guilty of. When I reach a goal in my life, I instinctively point to someone who is doing something even more incredible, minimising my achievements and making myself feel small.

That day in West Sussex, gripping my beech nut mast, I decide to use the hours of silence I will experience on the trail to let myself feel all the losses in my life, without reference to other people's suffering.

I linger near the back of the group as we walk.

I am not here to win a race, to be the first. I want to feel every step I take.

Soon we pass a memorial to a Polish fighter pilot called Bolesław Andrzej Własnowolski, who died at the tender age of twenty-three when his Hurricane was shot down in the Battle of Britain. I think instantly of my granny and her lost love. At my mum's funeral, one of the congregation had described her as a hurricane and I've since been given that same appellation at times. I smile at the memories. I would have missed this moment had I been running ahead.

I expect my mind to be filled with more of these recol-
lections, but for the most part I just listen and observe the
natural world around me. The slurping sounds my boots
make as I enter a muddy path under some trees and wade
through a few centimetres of standing water. The calls of
curious robins shouting at me for attention. With no one
speaking, the only competition to the birdsong is the
harmony that plays out as the wind rustles the leaves on
the trees.

We are walking to Kingley Vale – a nature reserve and
Site of Special Scientific Interest, famed for its impressive
collection of yew trees, some of the oldest in England.

But first we climb to the top of the earthworks on Bow
Hill to get a bigger picture.

As well as being referred to as the Devil's Humps, these
round barrows are also known as the King's Graves.
Folklore tells of the men of nearby Chichester, our destination, defending the region against Viking warriors. The
defeated Viking leaders, the story goes, lie buried under
these mounds. The trees that line the slopes below us are
said to be their foot-soldiers who transformed into a forest
in defeat. Some claim that they come to life here after dark,
re-treading old ground.

I have been here before, sleeping out in hammocks
strung between these wooded ghosts for a radio programme
with only the producer, Charlotte, for company. It had been

a new experience for me, sharing the wilderness with a woman. We talked, toasted marshmallows and laughed well into the night. Then slept soundly untroubled by spirits, before being woken by a small fawn that had wandered into the circle of branches in which we lay.

Standing on the top of the barrows now, I gaze along an ancient ridgeway, one of a network of the UK's oldest forms of roads, which meanders towards the sea. We do not follow it, and instead walk downhill, heading towards the yew tree grove.

Daylight significantly reduces as we move under the cover of the canopy. Wandering here, I remember the woods that stretched out behind my house growing up. We used to build dens amid the many oaks and sycamores, until the police warned there was a flasher lurking amid the darkness. Overnight that place of refuge was tainted with danger and we were forbidden from playing there.

Fairy tales always like to set disturbing stories amid old trees. From an early age we are meant to fear that which we cannot see. I find it intriguing that the serpent in the Garden of Eden was found amid the branches of a tree. Red Riding Hood is attacked in the forest by a wolf, Hansel and Gretel get lost and succumb to the entrapment of a witch deep inside woodland, and even the Gruffalo – a strange and deformed beast much loved by children – lurks in the 'deep dark wood'.

Yet I find such darkened nooks comforting; they provide me with a secret place to disappear.

The thing that makes these particular trees so special is their age. Not because a yew shouldn't last that long, but because many of them were used to make English long-bows back in the fourteenth century and became so desirable that a government 'yew tax' was introduced, and people went in search of forests like this one to harvest the wood for free. How it survived is a mystery.

I walk around the wizened arms of one specimen and run my fingers over its rough bark. These trees are so difficult to age – as they grow, their central core rots away – but from the girth of their trunks it's easy to believe that these specimens may predate Christianity.

Pagans used to associate yew with death and rebirth. Death because of the great age of many of them, their rotting core and red berries that are poisonous to humans; rebirth because they can drop a low branch to the ground and from that grow a whole new tree. Even when the Christian faith gained hold, the yew tree still held a powerful link to life and death and was used to mark graveyards and churches – explaining why it is still seen in many today.

There are lots of theories about why the yew has a close association with Christian religious sites. Did they act as a barrier to stop farmers grazing animals in cemeteries (the berries are poisonous to them too)? Or was the aim to prevent archers from cutting them for bows (as they would never poach in a holy place)? I once read that a yew tree would outlast an iron post of the same age. There is something quite magical in that.

Whatever the initial reason, these trees began to symbolise resurrection in the Christian faith. And as I stand here, leaning on one of the oldest in the country, I think about the life I am beginning to build anew after so many years thinking it was already over.

At first we played it cool, my paramedic and I. Neither of us wanted to appear too eager. He had come out of a long-term relationship that had stopped working and had experienced a few false starts with other girlfriends in the time that followed. We realised we'd moved to Berkshire in the same year a decade ago to start a new chapter in our lives. We undoubtedly passed each other in the supermarket, but never knew our lives would become intertwined.

On our second date we started walking in the dark, on an absurd mission to find a highly recommended pizza in a pub several kilometres away.

We wandered amid the trees of a place called Common Wood in High Wycombe. Semi-natural and consisting of oak, aspen, ash and fir, it is also stocked with lots of beech trees, planted long ago when this town was a centre for furniture building.

In the dark we stumbled over fallen branches, crossed pathways, climbed over the rails of a road, and finally made it to the hostelry to claim our edible prize. I didn't hold back from eating, nor did I feel guilty about being hungry again.

On our way back we kissed beneath the bough of a yew, while scurrying sounds indicated badgers and roe deer were close. Tawny owls called in the darkness and he asked me if I knew that the 'twit-twoo' sound they made was actually a harmony between a male and female bird rather than one lonely soul.

I looked into his eyes and allowed myself to feel content.

Shortly after Kingley Vale's grove of trees we reach West Stoke Church, where Abigail leads us inside and we each light our candle from hers. Inside the building, any sound is amplified and I am very aware of any sniffs and snuffles made by my fellow pilgrims.

We were told that the vicar would try and meet us here to offer us a blessing on our way. But he doesn't come and so we silently leave, blowing out our candles, and continue on our way.

This walk is not a long one – I would once have run the same distance within an hour – but, as I wander, I realise that I no longer feel the need to prove myself on the long hard routes that once I felt I had to endure. I still like a challenge, but one I have chosen, on my own terms, for my own reasons, rather than blindly following a route or plan that someone else has told me I should.

We begin to break through into the boundaries of the city of Chichester, whose cathedral is our final goal. But first, we reach Brandy Hole Copse, another patch of trees. Here my mind wanders freely as I try to locate the blue tits I can hear in song. I notice a patch of wood fungi clustering on the bark of a tree, and smell the distinct dampness of marsh ground somewhere amid the many sweet chestnuts.

Emerging onto the Centurion Way, we cross an old Roman Road. The sounds of songbirds are replaced by the call of the gulls. The temperature has dropped amid the dusk and I place my hands into my pockets to warm them. As I do, I feel a prick on one of my fingertips, and remember my intention, the beech mast that I had placed here at the start.

While exploring pilgrim paths in Britain, I was also sent to Norway, to walk a few sections of the St Olav's Way, a recently rediscovered pilgrim route from the eleventh century, founded by then King Olav, who had been chased out of his country for trying to unite it under one crown (his) and one religion (Christianity). While there I met with a priest in one of the churches, a man called Frede Fjågesundto. I asked him why he thought we'd seen a resurgence of so many pilgrim paths around the world. His answer was that the way people express their beliefs has fundamentally changed. 'We sit in offices and work on computers all day – not using our bodies,' he said. 'So walking a pilgrimage is perhaps more of a need than it ever was.'

On some level his answer made sense. We are more sedentary than we ever have been – there's an alarming finding recently published that school-aged children in Britain now spend less time outside than prison inmates. Yet for me, I don't believe it is just the physical expression of a belief. It is something much deeper.

As we near the huge imposing structure of the cathedral ahead, Abigail gestures towards a gate, and we enter the Bishop's Palace Gardens. Here, manicured plants sit within the old city walls and we walk onto their ramparts, looking down on what would have presumably once been a moat.

We stand still and wait as Abigail pulls out her intention and throws it over the side of the wall. She gestures for us to do the same – a symbolic action of leaving behind the problems we've carried with us on this journey, removing the burden on our backs.

I look down at the spiky husk in my hand. I've only picked it up this morning, yet I know that I've been carrying what it represents a whole lot longer.

Under the light of the moon, I throw it away and listen for its landing. It is too tiny in the vastness that lies beneath us to hear it, but I know it has reached its destination.

As we shuffle towards the cathedral we hope to catch Evensong. We are ushered into the main hall and take our positions in the pews, opposite a choir who are all dressed in long white robes.

I look at the faces of my companions. Each one has an expression that makes me wonder at what stage of their journeys they are at. Have they had their questions answered? Are they now formulating different ones? Are they about to embark on new beginnings, as I am?

I know I will never get the answer.

Just then a hush spreads among the cloisters and everyone looks about in anticipation. I realise I am holding my breath.

Then, from behind me, I hear the solo voice of a young boy singing the opening lines to 'Once in Royal David's City'. I think of my mum and my granny in a bittersweet rush. I remember the men from relationships past – all lost to me, but still, somewhere in the world, making their own way. Each one is etched on my mind like carvings on beech bark. I think of the anguish with my dad in moments past, and the healing conversations we've begun to have lately. I picture secret photographs and controlling messages, I think of new love, a new journey and all the risks that brings with it.

Then, I think of nothing at all.

Instead, I open my mouth and finally, somehow, find my voice.

And I sing.

I, Pilgrim

I am following the trail of a brimstone butterfly as it draws me along the riverside. Slowly I move, watching its delicate flutterings among the scrub at the water's edge. I envy its apparent weightlessness. On my back, I'm carrying over 10 kilograms, which will only become heavier over time.

The river I am walking along is the Thames, the second longest river in Britain, which makes its way from a lonely field in Gloucestershire out towards the east, passing through another eight counties and two cities – including London – before eventually joining the sea in Essex. I'm on assignment again, walking a 100-kilometre section of the Thames Path, which is celebrating turning twenty-five.

But I am also, unexpectedly, walking a pilgrim path. Rivers were sacred to ancient peoples well before Christianity spread. They were the source of life, providing water to drink as well as bountiful food in both vegetation and sea life. I once went foraging with an instructor who told me that if she had to live in the early days of man she would choose to be by water, as you would then have the best chance to survive. As such, early humans would make offerings to this river thanking mother nature for her great bounty.

Amid the resurgence in popularity of pilgrim paths, a reverend in the diocese of Oxford decided to mark the end of his ministry as bishop by inaugurating a ten-day route following the path on which I now find myself walking, which he named The Thames Pilgrim Way.

It doesn't start at the source of the river and it doesn't end at the sea. Instead, it begins at the western edge of the diocese in Radcot, Oxfordshire, and finishes at the eastern boundary in Wraysbury, Berkshire. Along the way it passes a number of priories, cathedrals and churches.

Religion, I have come to realise, is woven into our lives whether we are religious or not. The saints provide the names of the streets we walk along to work and form the basis for our calendar of public holidays. Like multiple narratives strung across the warp of a loom, or indeed the lines that span the body of a scallop shell, they are at the basic level the fabric of many societies, linking everything together.

For me this is an 'accidental pilgrimage' and its timing is pretty apt. My life has once again changed significantly.

Snores from over my shoulder indicate to me that my heavy load is asleep. He's just about to turn nine months and his presence still occasionally surprises me. Like all the best pilgrimages, life has led me in an unexpected direction.

I didn't intend to become pregnant. In fact, there were many reasons why I believed I couldn't. So for the first few months I just thought I was ill – lethargic, nauseous and tender. Once more the world seemed to have conspired to take one of my major life-changing events and minimise it against the backdrop of a global problem. As if things didn't feel fractured enough after Brexit, the Covid pandemic had taken hold. I was still on assignments right up until I caught the virus myself: skiing, drinking, diving, throwing myself into life with a new partner, the paramedic I had met on my kayak. Then, life came to a crashing halt. Everything I thought I knew disappeared overnight. I could not travel. I could not work. And now I was ill.

When I took the pregnancy test I thought it must be wrong – a cheap one for under a pound could surely not be reliable. But the doctor told me they are all the same. I had to make a choice about what to do next.

I hadn't been with my partner long, just a few months. We both felt lost.

I visited the pregnancy advisory clinic where other women sat in similar predicaments. There's a lot of judgement bandied around about the question we were all asking ourselves ('can I do this?'), and especially in religious circles. But I found the clinic to be a place of love and understanding. Before you are even allowed to consider your options, you have a counselling session with a wonderful woman who will speak with you as long as needed and even see you multiple times. You cannot have anyone else in the room with you. The decision has to be yours; they want to check you are not being coerced.

There is no agenda. No one wants anything other than what you want. In the waiting room was a mix of people. A young student couple who had made a mistake and sat holding hands, feeling guilty but knowing they were not in any position to continue. A teenage girl with her mum. A woman dressed in an abaya still clutching her luggage with a tag on it from Heathrow Airport.

Everyone's situation was different, and it is not my place to judge them, or myself for being there. After my visit I went for a walk and spent the day in a woodland, drinking tea in the rain and splashing in puddles.

Without the clinic I don't think I'd have had the strength or the information to make a decision. I am forever grateful for their support.

I decide to take a break to eat some lunch alongside a boathouse on the outskirts of Abingdon. My son stirs in his carrier, his ever-smiling face round and cherubic. It's a hot day and I find us shade beneath the boughs of a hornbeam tree.

I've now been alive for longer without my mother than I've known life with her. In my baby's face I see flashes of her. I named him after her family, only later finding out that the word meant 'blessed'.

Being pregnant in lockdown was hard. Especially as me and my partner were only just getting to know each other. His work for the Air Ambulance naturally never stopped. While I was housebound, my wings were clipped and my career faltered. Every chance I got I went outside. My daily walk took me off-grid, away from any other people. Often I would choose to go at night so I was free to wander away from prying eyes.

No one I worked with knew I was pregnant; I hid it from the world, not wanting them to see me any differently, before I was ready to see myself that way too.

In the heatwave that came I longed for water. With all public pools closed and no sign of re-opening, I started swimming in the river that I'm now walking alongside – the same river on which I first met my son's father.

My body changed in pregnancy, all the sharp edges slowly became round. My face, always so pale and the source of much teasing in school, was now regularly flushed red as though I were drunk.

When I was eight months pregnant and travel restrictions had begun to ease, I went home to Wales. I couldn't stay with my dad, who was classed as 'vulnerable', so I climbed to the top of Mum's mountain and slept in the folds of its flanks to feel her warm embrace.

The pandemic was both a blessing and a curse. I couldn't travel, but suddenly everyone was prevented from doing it too, not just me because I was growing a human in my belly. Everyone was questioning their chosen pathway and I heard of people I knew well losing and quitting jobs on a near-daily basis. It was hard, but the time did give me space. To think about my future and to watch in awe as my son developed, inch by inch, away from anyone's gaze or judgement.

When I first saw him on the ultrasound, he seemed to dance in my womb, unaware of the confines he sat within, unknowing of the whole world that awaited him and the many paths we would wander, both together and apart.

Now, as we sit on the bank, he drinks his milk and babbles in appreciation, while I lie on the grass and try to stretch out my aching back.

The churches on this route are plentiful. I don't have the official guide to this spiritual pathway, no information about the saints associated with it. But looking on the Ordnance Survey map I can see a cluster of buildings of many different denominations in the town ahead.

The day before my child was born, I climbed a hill in the Chilterns. I was heavy and tired of carrying the extra weight. On the way back I fell, tumbling a few metres down a slope. Instinctively I used my hands to protect him. My trousers ripped and the skin on my legs was grazed and bleeding. Then a red kite emerged from behind the mound and whistled in song.

The next day I went into labour, in the midst of writing. Covid rules meant I would have to go in alone if I went to the hospital too early, so I spent the first few hours of contractions dictating my thoughts to my partner, who dutifully typed them in a strange kind of awe.

Between each surge of pain, there would be nothing, as though the whole thing had been a bad dream. Then it would start again until it became constant and the gaps in between seemed to disappear.

They say a woman forgets the pain of childbirth after she's had her baby, but that hasn't happened to me. I remember it clearly. I wonder if others do too but are afraid to be the ones who counter the well-established assertion.

After Abingdon we head further along the river, passing the abbey at Dorchester, though I am more drawn to the clumps at Wittenham – on top of which the oldest planted cluster of beech trees in England sit, known as the Cuckoo Pen. It's said that if that bird is captured and held here it will ensure an eternal summer.

At Wallingford, I trade church visits to walk amid the footprint of an old castle, whose bricks were said to have been taken to build the royal residence at Windsor.

My favourite stop comes at the edge of a village called Cholsey. It's here that I used to swim when pregnant, with a friend I met through my partner whose son is a month younger than mine. In the last month of my pregnancy we both paddle-boarded to an island not far from here, and spent the night in the coolness of the outdoors, listening to geese call and seeing the occasional kingfisher dart by in a flash of electric blue.

Now my son watches a group of older boys as they frolic in the shallows. He screams with delight and starts motioning as though he's splashing in the bath.

I had wanted to deliver him in a pool, wanted his transition into this world to go from one liquid to another. But every time I got into it, my body began to relax too much and labour slowed down.

Giving birth was raw and primal. I found strength I never knew existed. I found kinship with all the women who had done this before me and will do it when I've long ceased to exist.

Between contractions I found myself remembering a visit to Western Australia in the middle of the Kimberley, a wilderness region known for its beauty as much as its danger. Frequently, roads are washed out by flash floods, people who run out of fuel can wait for days to be rescued, and a lack of mobile coverage means there is no way of calling for help. At one site I visited I was taken to an old rock, known by the aboriginal community as a 'birthing stone'. It is said that women, when it was time, would come here and stand, clutching this sandstone in the throes of labour, holding the hand of their ancestors who are part of the land. There's a cleaved mould on this rock and I ran my fingers over it to feel a connection with the women from centuries ago.

All those years before, when I first arrived at the cathedral of Santiago, I had read about the long-standing tradition of pilgrims entering the stone Portico de la Gloria and resting their hand on the central column where St James stands. There are deep grooves within it, left from the millions of travellers who have stood there and done this before. The practice allowed pilgrims to feel a physical connection with them. Yet this practice was banned by the cathedral in recent years and I never got to do it. Instead, you are encouraged to embrace a gilded statue of the saint from behind, in the central part of the cathedral, feeling like you are desperately trying to win the acknowledgement of an uninterested father.

Not getting to do it had haunted me for years; I always felt that something lay incomplete about my journey there. Yet touching that rock in Australia a few years later had seemed much more powerful.

Going through childbirth, at times almost watching myself as though from the other side of the room, while I knelt down and pushed my body to its limits, I realised that it really didn't matter.

It took fourteen hours of labour for me to meet my son; fourteen hours lost to my most animalistic state. The midwives who I was most scared of before, such was their overwhelming maternal symbolism, fought for me, and I was glad of them.

At Goring we stop to sleep in a coach house opposite a church. As it's Wednesday night, normally the bell-ringers would be practising, their chimes risking waking the baby, but it's August so there is a break from the tradition. I fall asleep instead to the sound of happy customers eating and drinking downstairs in the pub and the soft and steady breathing coming from the travel cot.

The town of Goring is on one side of the Thames in the county of Oxfordshire, and its twin, Streatley, sits opposite in Berkshire. This place is known as the Goring Gap, where the Chilterns are separated from the Berkshire Downs by the river that flows between them, which, over time, caused a valley to form.

Once more, I feel as though my life has been divided. Whereas before I looked back at my time as either 'before Mum died' and 'after she was gone', now I see a split of myself 'before being a parent' and 'life after'.

This change has impacted every facet of my life anew. Some friends have abandoned me to motherhood, taking no interest in the unexpected direction my life has turned. Several work colleagues have also written me off, assuming that I will no longer be capable of travel due to my incumbent 'baggage'. My hair – once soft and thick from pregnancy hormones – has fallen out in clumps. My face is permanently red and spotted with rosacea. From countless sleepless nights, wrinkles have begun to form around my eyes, and my conversation is temporarily stunted, my world now a blur of babyisms.

I've been left with an underactive thyroid, the gland that's in your throat shaped like a butterfly, which controls all the hormones and metabolism to keep your body alive. Mine can no longer be left to regulate itself without aid. And the rest of my body – over which I once grasped so much control – has grown and swelled in ways I couldn't stop. Curves I liked have become rounded wobbly bumps, my belly refuses to flatten as it was before. I have developed a painful condition in the tendons of my wrists from breastfeeding and carrying my boy, which means I am in constant agony, a pain that no one can see. I look on social media and see other women who are adventurers like me and have had babies – sometimes multiple – and have managed to 'bounce back' into the shape they resembled before. Yet I remain stubbornly as I was when with child.

But I don't care. Where friends left, others arrived, and I am sure even some of my older ones will return. Work may well change but I will change with it, seek out other opportunities, explore new pathways I never considered before. I have learned I need to make time to take care of myself, to treat my body as well as my mind, to take my tablets and not see a medical diagnosis as a weakness. I accept now that my body has changed and will change again, and though it will never be as it was before, neither will I, and that is also, in many ways, a good thing.

As we walk beyond Goring, bound for Pangbourne, my rounded belly spills over the waistband of my rucksack. Yet I am not sad. I am no longer scared that the photos I sent to The Scientist will be revealed. And even if they are, the woman who appears in them no longer exists. She is like a painted icon in a church, a figure from the past who has ceased to walk among us. I remember her now, as though an old friend who walked in another direction from the way I am now headed.

The heat has become too much, so I find respite at St Mary's Church in Whitchurch. The doors are locked, so we sit on the stone steps outside, shaded from the sun. I eat a sandwich while my son feasts on blended carrots, which he somehow manages to wipe all over his forehead as though he's been christened by orange liquid. There's a note on the metal gate advising that regular services are no longer as common as they were before Covid.

Since the pandemic, churches have had to change and adapt. Mass communion was forbidden, weddings banned, and services were forced to take place virtually instead. Congregation numbers were already dwindling pre-pandemic, but pilgrim routes were growing and the paths themselves could, of course, not be closed. Perhaps the priest in Norway was right: if the Church wants to guarantee its future, it must escape the confines of an old building that no longer fits its purpose.

I put my boy back into the baby carrier and swing it onto my torso. He giggles as though I've told a funny joke and babbles as we cross a toll bridge that still charges vehicles a fee to cross it.

In Pangbourne we see a flurry of people congregated near the lock. A whole flotilla of skiffs is gathered, the occupants wearing regal red jackets bearing standards with coats of arms. This is the annual Swan Upping, a process dating back at least eight hundred years when swan meat was considered a culinary delicacy and a sign of wealth if it were served on your table. To buy it meant purchasing an astronomically expensive 'mark' from the government. To protect them as a commodity the Crown declared that all unmarked swans belonged to them and began a yearly tradition of rowing the river to divide them between their owners.

Nowadays they are not eaten, but the ceremony is still performed over five days, taking the form of a wildlife census to check on the health of the birds and count their numbers, and see if any environmental impacts are affecting the population.

It seems to be a good example of a rich man's tradition of showcasing ownership slowly morphing into something more beneficial to everyone, including the natural world. It gives me hope.

People I pass are quick to comment on my load. I'm called 'crazy' and 'brave' in equal measure. Yet taking my baby for a walk – whether on a trail or a pilgrim path – seems to me to be neither. It is in fact necessary. I am constantly evolving, and walking as I do gives me time and space to evaluate who it is I am at that moment.

I didn't expect my story to end this way. This isn't my moment of salvation. I wasn't a childless woman hoping to become a mother. I wasn't a vessel waiting to fulfil my biological destiny. I am not the Virgin Mary clutching her saviour in a swaddle. But perhaps all I have been through means that in some small way I can be my son's.

I have once again stumbled onto an unmarked path, one I never intended to tread. I am on a winter mountain-top breaking trail. I don't know where it leads next.

The Thames Path cuts through the town of Reading and immediately the idyllic country scene gives way to the urban. I hear more car horns than goose honks. At King's Meadow someone has retrieved a scooter from the bottom of the river and it stands on the river bank, encased in mud, like some kind of modern art installation.

I pass a gate within which the metal has been forged into two crossed oars. At Sonning I take the bridge over the river as the route switches bank sides, but I do not venture to see the church. It is too far for me and I do not want to leave the trail I'm on.

I spy the island where I recently took my dad camping for the first time and wish I got to see him more often. Then I notice a black swan, its red eyes glowing ominously. Research has shown that, on average, a quarter of them are gay, often forming threesomes until the female breeds, then stealing her eggs and raising them as their own. Life, even in the animal kingdom, is never straightforward.

Soon after, I reach the café where the first serendipitous meeting with my partner saw me join this path that I am now walking upon.

We stop at Henley and I check into a hotel that was once a brewery, the barrels now replaced with rolltop baths, the pipework now funnelling warm water to heat the floors. While my son rests I think of my mum and wish she had lived to know my baby. When I look at him peacefully sleeping, appearing more content than I believe I have ever felt in my life, I worry that something unexpected will happen to me. If I cease to exist my son won't get to know me, in the same way I feel I didn't really get to know my own mother. We were only just reaching the stage in our lives when we were evolving from parent and child to something more profound. It was the start of what I hoped would be a great, lifelong friendship.

'Mum' was a word I once winced at, yet now it has become my name, and I wait patiently for the day my son will call me by it.

I'm on the final stretch of my walk now. I leave the hotel while it is still dark. I am weary but know that if I put in one long day I can reach my house before sunset.

A sign in the grass tells me I am at the start line of the famous Henley Regatta, a regatta that sees boat crews compete for glory on this stretch of the water, which has been held here since 1839.

Rain begins to fall and I pull out the cover to shelter my son from the sting of raindrops.

Despite my slow pace, my life is still moving pretty fast, much like the Botafumeiro in the cathedral of Santiago that so captured my attention. But there has been a change in me. Even with the commitment of being a mother, I no longer feel trapped by confinements.

I look over to the water where a grebe darts beneath the surface to explore a new world beneath.

I have stopped trying to live up to others' expectations. Rather, I have become something more like a river. Somehow consistent and constant, even if still capable of surprising. There is always the possibility that I will change my course, that life will construct a damn or a weir or a diversion. But I know now that I can, given time, overcome it.

The path takes me away from the water temporarily and I am thrust into a field of long grass. Between its stalks tower the lilac pom-poms of field scabious – a plant once used by herbalists to treat skin conditions – as well as the white splashes of Queen Anne's lace or 'wild carrot', often seen as a symbol of purity, wisdom and sanctuary. There's also the occasional yellow ragwort, aptly known as St James' wort – poisonous to some, though loved by butterflies and bees.

When we reach Medmenham my son is asleep so I cannot show him the Egyptian geese sitting by the water, nursing their fluffy cluster of five chicks. I want to stop and rest, but now he's settled I resolve to keep moving so as not to disturb his routine.

As I continue on, I recall one of the only memories I have from living in England as a child. My mum could drive a car, but instead she bought a bicycle and a fold-down seat that she could strap me or my brother into and race around the town at speed. I remember she would take me to Latchford Swing Bridge, which spanned the point where the River Mersey meets the Manchester Ship Canal. She would beg for us to be able to 'ride' on it as it rotated out into the channel, cutting off the road at both sides, allowing ships to pass by.

At Hurley I pass what was once a Benedictine priory – what remains of it now part of a private residence – and the Olde Bell pub and hotel, claimed by some to be the oldest in the world, that once served the priory before the Reformation.

When I reach Bisham and spot the square shape of All Saint's Church across the water, along with the manor house that stands where once there was an Augustine abbey, the rain has lessened to a drizzle. I think back to all I have learned about the saints and the Church and pilgrimage in our country.

It seems strange to me that history and religion are still taught as distinct subjects, yet really they are forever entwined. Perhaps if they were more commonly taught together, rather than stand-alone, to show their interlinking impact, everyone would be more open-minded. The one overriding thing I've learned is that every path, no matter how far away it seems from the one I'm on, has an unexpected link with another.

I know that I had to walk old paths in order to discover new trails. It's the real reason I think people are walking these pilgrim routes so often today. We are re-making lost connections, seeking to understand what joins where we are now to what has happened in the past. And we find some comfort in that.

It's said that when the last abbot of the now replaced abbey here on the Thames was removed during its dissolution in the sixteenth century, he placed a curse on all future owners so that they may 'be hounded by misfortune'. Even now I can understand his anger and upset. Endings, I've learned, are usually always hard and that's because they aren't ever really an ending at all, more a new beginning either sought out or thrust upon us.

My son begins to squirm, eager to escape the confines of his carrier. I try to soothe him, tell him it's not far to go. He settles a little, but by the time I reach Bourne End (from the phrase 'burn end') – a place named after the actual terminus of the River Wye – we stop, and I take him out and allow him some freedom. He still can't move too fast, though he likes to crawl through the damp grass and discover new textures against his skin.

In a sense, young children are like sponges, soaking up the world around them with an unrivalled energy. Though I know full well he won't remember this walk, I like to think that the things he's seen, heard and touched will resonate with him in the future, even if I don't get to be a part of all of it.

I sit between him and the water, which is moving as slowly as he is. I smile. Pilgrimage has helped me realise that it's okay to slow down. Life doesn't need to constantly rush by at speed to feel exciting. My son develops slowly but subtly; with each day there is a new sound he can make or a new action he can take. And it's this subtlety of the change, the constantly shifting ebb and flow, that is far more sustainable and satisfying.

He climbs onto my legs and I tickle his chin with a buttercup. All this time I have been seeking guidance through religious footpaths, but all along my altar has been nature and I a devoted disciple.

The rain has long gone, yet the sun has not appeared. Instead, a thick haze lingers, and the atmosphere feels heavy and close. Still I continue on, determined I will not cheat myself out of walking back to my own front door. Soon I pass through Cookham, then on to the riverside at Maidenhead. Here a group of rowdy teenage girls are arguing. Someone has crossed a line and revenge is being threatened.

I sing to my son to distract him from the furore and he rewards my many musical notes by joining in with excited squeals and babbles.

Home is near now. On this section the path has temporarily finished its winding around corners that I cannot see. I'm walking back to a place I feel I belong, to a man who loves me, with a happy companion on my back, my own new beginning.

I know I cannot continue forever on this current straight line. There will be future losses, betrayals, lies, deceit and pain – because life is not one easy pathway. But along the way there will also be love and laughter, unexpected joy and the thrill of exhilaration, and many moments – big and small – that seem magical just for a few fleeting seconds.

The trees seem to line our route like a sabre arch outside a church wedding. I feel my pace quicken as I wander outside Bray, where I will leave the river to take the bridge into town and find my front door. I will not pass any famous chapels, but I do wander alongside a cemetery, the resting place of those whose long pilgrimage is finally over.

As I walk, a flock of Canada geese flies overhead in the shape of a V. They are not a native species to the UK, though these particular ones will have been born here and only know this place as home. Like me, they never really belonged in one place or the other. Yet with their flock, flying high with others like them, they are strong and thrive. My son tries to mimic their calls.

I am still not religious. But I do believe that life is a pilgrimage to an eventual and inevitable end. Hopefully I still have a long way to go on mine, and on it I will approach the upcoming obstacles with a different spring in my step. When things get hard, I do not pray. A Catholic friend I had in high school said her mum would only allow me to come over for tea as long as I believed in a being higher than myself, one I could talk to. I didn't go. But now I would.

For me, that being is my mum. I never understood before these pilgrimages how much losing her had impacted me at every level, in every relationship and every phase of my life. Now that I know, I won't shy away from that loss. Because it isn't all loss. Instead, in many ways, I feel I have gained something that others don't have. When I need clarity I climb to the top of a mountain, stand on the edge of a sea cliff, or follow a river home. I can commune with her without saying a single word. And, sometimes, she answers. She is the flutter of a butterfly that I follow, the wind that softly brushes my hair from my cheek, or the call of a bird who makes my heart sing.

And I follow her now, to my new home. The place where I shall begin, again.

Acknowledgements

Writing this book has felt like a pilgrimage in itself, with many bends in the trail that I didn't always see coming and obstacles presented that I didn't know how to find my way around. Thankfully, I wasn't alone and have the privilege of knowing some very special people who could help me navigate my way forward. There are a great many souls who have been vital on my journey – way more than I can list here, but I will try my best.

First, I'd like to thank my family for letting me tell my truth unhindered. Re-treading this old ground has been tough for me, as it will be for you reading it, but knowing I had your full support when I did allowed me to be able to write with truth and honesty and that has made all the difference. Dad and Tom – thank you for being part of my ongoing journey.

To my partner Andy and son B, you have changed my entire world and I love you both for it. Thank you for understanding every time I need to undertake a solo journey, and for always being there to welcome me back home with endless hugs and kisses.

My literary agent Caroline Montgomery has stuck with me from when this idea was a passing thought, through the several missteps and false summits, until we got to this point on the pathway. Thank you to you Caro, and your mum – the late, great Doreen – for finally pushing me to commit this story to paper.

To Jonathan de Peyer at HarperNorth (and the HarperCollins team – Gen, Alice, Hilary, Meg and Tas), thank you for pursuing me and asking me to write this book on what at the time must have felt like a wing and a prayer. I'm so glad I waited until now and that you were the ones to turn it into an actual book. My story is all the better for it.

I owe a huge debt of gratitude to the K Blundell Trust, without whom I could not have afforded the necessary childcare to enable me to finish this book during the final stages. Thanks so much for honouring me with the grant, and thanks to the Society of Authors for making me feel I deserve a place among so many talented writers.

A massive heartfelt thanks to the British Pilgrimage Trust, not only for allowing me to come on their walks, but for committing to creating an ever-growing database of all the pilgrim pathways in Britain, free of charge, for those of us who seek some guidance. Thanks to their wonderful guides Guy and Abigail; to the participants who gave their time and spoke to me when I asked; and, of course, to Will, who set me on the quest that enabled me to find my voice again and sing.

When I was writing this book, The Coach House in Dorchester, The Crest in Bournemouth, and the Gladstone Library in Hawarden were key sanctuaries, locked away from my hectic life. Thank you for the space.

Thanks to Libby, Claire and Daniel, for helping with B when I needed to take time out from being 'mum' to gain some time to write.

For Sophie, who called me that night in the woods, and John who took me on the adventure that not only gave me a much-needed focus but also started me on a whole new path in my life. And for Danny who asked me the question I needed to be confronted with. You know you each saved me – thank you forever.

I have spent the last two years revisiting many of these footpaths with a clearer head, on research trips, sometimes with friends who came to keep me company. I'd like to thank them all, including Ben, Mel and Finn on Iona; Tim at Trail Outlaws; Patrick Norris at Footsteps in Northumberland (your stories on the sand truly brought the place back to life); Polly, Luke, Max and Elsie in Essex; Marina and Elaine in Northern Ireland (I am so pleased that your prayers were answered after we met); Gaynor for lending me her book in Danby; and all the pilgrims I met on my travels.

An ongoing thanks to Jane at the *Guardian* for allowing me to write for you; and to Julia Spence (and team), Inntravel and Ben at the *Telegraph* for sending me to walk my last – unplanned – pilgrimage with my son.

A solid 'high five' and big hug to Dwayne, my friend and teammate, who walked the length of Britain with me and trusted me enough to share his story with me so that I felt I could begin to share mine. I will always have your back, as you have mine. We did it.

Huge love to Lottie (and Arty the dog) for allowing me to complain endlessly about book writing on our walks, and then allowing me to offer help when your own wonderful mum went to join mine.

To Sue for your non-judgemental hugs, understanding and hot chocolates following the affair with The Scientist; it meant so very much.

And to all the readers of my words for contacting me and encouraging me to keep writing, even when I thought I couldn't. I can't name you all but please know that your support gives me strength.

Last, but by no means least, love, respect and gratitude endlessly to Cerys. You welcomed me into your family when I felt most alone and allowed me to share the joy of teaching your children about the wonders of the outdoors. You made me a good mum before I ever became one officially. Your friendship, loyalty, unwavering support and sage advice has supported me better than any pilgrim staff. Here's to our continuing adventures on the trail ahead. This is just the beginning ...

Harper North

Book Credits

HarperNorth would like to thank the following staff and
contributors for their involvement in making
this book a reality:

Fionnuala Barrett

Samuel Birkett

Peter Borcsok

Ciara Briggs

Sarah Burke

Matthew Burne

Fiona Cooper

Alan Cracknell

Jonathan de Peyer

Anna Derkacz

Tom Dunstan

Kate Elton

Sarah Emsley

Nick Fawcett

Simon Gerratt

Lydia Grainge

Neil Gower

Monica Green

Natassa Hadjinicolaou

Megan Jones

Jean-Marie Kelly

Taslima Khatun

Sammy Luton

Petra Moll

Anna Morrison

Alice Murphy-Pyle

Adam Murray

Genevieve Pegg

James Ryan

Florence Shepherd

Eleanor Slater

Emma Sullivan

Katrina Troy

Daisy Watt

For more unmissable reads,
sign up to the HarperNorth newsletter at
www.harpernorth.co.uk

or find us on Twitter at
@HarperNorthUK

Harper
North